INHALANTS

by Hal Marcovitz

LUCENT BOOKS

An imprint of Thomson Gale, a part of The Thomson Corporation

THOMSON
™
GALE

Detroit • New York • San Francisco • San Diego • New Haven, Conn.
Waterville, Maine • London • Munich

THOMSON
————★————™
GALE

For more information, contact
Lucent Books
27500 Drake Rd.
Farmington Hills, MI 48331-3535
Or you can visit our Internet site at http://www.gale.com

LIBRARY OF CONGRESS CATALOGING-IN-PUBLICATION DATA

Marcovitz, Hal.
  Inhalants / by Hal Marcovitz.
    p. cm. — (Drug education library)
  Includes bibliographical references and index.
  ISBN 1-59018-416-5 (hard cover : alk. paper)
  1. Solvent abuse—Juvenile literature. I. Title. II. Series.
  RC568.S64M365 2005
  362.29'9—dc22

                                                            2005007465

Contents

Foreword

The development of drugs and drug use in America is a cultural paradox. On the one hand, strong, potentially dangerous drugs provide people with relief from numerous physical and psychological ailments. Sedatives like Valium counter the effects of anxiety; steroids treat severe burns, anemia, and some forms of cancer; morphine provides quick pain relief. On the other hand, many drugs (sedatives, steroids, and morphine among them) are consistently misused or abused. Millions of Americans struggle each year with drug addictions that overpower their ability to think and act rationally. Researchers often link drug abuse to criminal activity, traffic accidents, domestic violence, and suicide.

These harmful effects seem obvious today. Newspaper articles, medical papers, and scientific studies have highlighted the myriad problems drugs and drug use can cause. Yet, there was a time when many of the drugs now known to be harmful were actually believed to be beneficial. Cocaine, for example, was once hailed as a great cure, used to treat everything from nausea and weakness to colds and asthma. Developed in Europe during the 1880s, cocaine spread quickly to the United States where manufacturers made it the primary ingredient in such everyday substances as cough medicines, lozenges, and tonics. Likewise, heroin, an opium derivative, became a popular painkiller during the late nineteenth century. Doctors and patients flocked to American drugstores to buy heroin, described as the optimal cure for even the worst coughs and chest pains.

As more people began using these drugs, though, doctors, legislators, and the public at large began to realize that they were more damaging than beneficial. After years of using heroin as a painkiller, for example, patients began asking their doctors for larger and stronger doses. Cocaine users reported dangerous side effects, including hallucinations and wild mood shifts. As a result, the U.S. government initiated more stringent regulation of many powerful and addictive drugs, and in some cases outlawed them entirely.

A drug's legal status is not always indicative of how dangerous it is, however. Some drugs known to have harmful effects can be purchased legally in the United States and elsewhere. Nicotine, a key ingredient in cigarettes, is known to be highly addictive. In an effort to meet their bodies' demands for nicotine, smokers expose themselves to lung cancer, emphysema, and other life-threatening conditions. Despite these risks, nicotine is legal almost everywhere.

Other drugs that cannot be purchased or sold legally are the subject of much debate regarding their effects on physical and mental health. Marijuana, sometimes described as a gateway drug that leads users to other drugs, cannot legally be used, grown, or sold in this country. However, some research suggests that marijuana is neither addictive nor a gateway drug and that it might actually benefit cancer and AIDS patients by reducing pain and encouraging failing appetites. Despite these findings and occasional legislative attempts to change the drug's status, marijuana remains illegal.

The Drug Education Library examines the paradox of drugs and drug use in America by focusing on some of the most commonly used and abused drugs or categories of drugs available today. By discussing objectively the many types of drugs, their intended purposes, their effects (both planned and unplanned), and the controversies surrounding them, the books in this series provide readers with an understanding of the complex role drugs and drug use play in American society. Informative sidebars, annotated bibliographies, and organizations to contact lists highlight the text and provide young readers with many opportunities for further discussion and research.

Introduction

Inhalants: The Silent Epidemic

The U.S. Substance Abuse and Mental Health Services Administration (SAMHSA) estimates that each month, more than three hundred thousand Americans get high by inhaling fumes from chemical substances. Those who engage in this practice are known as "huffers" (if they draw in the vapor through their mouths) or "sniffers" (if they draw it in through their noses). Although some adults use inhalants to get high, most abusers are between the ages of twelve and sixteen. Abuse of inhalants is so rarely spoken of, and yet so widespread, that Harvey Weiss, executive director of the National Inhalant Prevention Coalition, has labeled it the "silent epidemic."

The chemicals that inhalers abuse are found in ordinary household products, motor fuels, and similar substances. As such, they occupy a unique place in the drug culture because they are legal, inexpensive, and easily obtainable on the shelves of supermarkets, convenience stores, and other retailers. By contrast, drugs such as marijuana, cocaine, and heroin are illegal, costly, and relatively difficult for teenagers to obtain.

Inhalants are also easy to use. No rolling papers, homemade pipes, or intravenous needles are needed to achieve a high. Many

6

Although inhalants are dangerous, they are easily accessible in many homes. These teens are looking for chemicals to inhale among everyday products kept in the garage.

parents who think they are vigilant in keeping drugs out of the hands of their children do not pay attention to the dangers of the household cleaners under the sink, the tank of gasoline in the garage, or the canister of whipped cream in the refrigerator. "How would I know to look at a can of butane with fear?"[1] asked Toy Slayton, whose seventeen-year-old son Johnson died after huffing butane, a gas commonly used in lighter fluids and for other purposes.

Inhalant abuse is not just a problem in the United States. According to the European School Project on Alcohol and Other Drugs, 20 percent of British youths between the ages of twelve and sixteen have tried inhalants. In Sweden and Greece, studies show that more young people experiment with inhalants than with marijuana. Because inhalants are inexpensive and readily available, inhalant abuse has become common in poorer countries of Europe, Asia, and Africa. In Romania, for example, one study estimates that 74 percent of young people have tried inhalants.

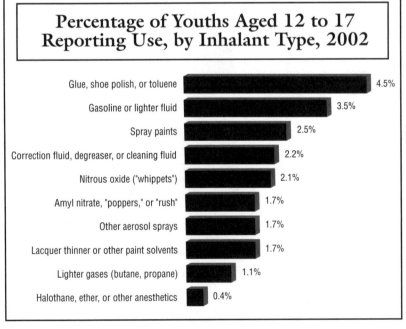

Percentage of Youths Aged 12 to 17 Reporting Use, by Inhalant Type, 2002

Inhalant Type	Percentage
Glue, shoe polish, or toluene	4.5%
Gasoline or lighter fluid	3.5%
Spray paints	2.5%
Correction fluid, degreaser, or cleaning fluid	2.2%
Nitrous oxide ("whippets")	2.1%
Amyl nitrate, "poppers," or "rush"	1.7%
Other aerosol sprays	1.7%
Lacquer thinner or other paint solvents	1.7%
Lighter gases (butane, propane)	1.1%
Halothane, ether, or other anesthetics	0.4%

Source: National Survey on Drug Use and Health

Each year, the U.S. government spends some $2 billion to combat drug abuse. The United States and other nations have signed treaties designed to wipe out foreign cocaine and opium production. U.S. Navy and Coast Guard ships patrol the seas in search of drug smugglers. Border patrols, often employing drug-sniffing dogs, inspect for narcotics in automobiles and trucks; customs officers examine the passengers and cargo of arriving airplanes. Local police departments regularly round up drug dealers and confiscate millions of dollars in illegal substances. Once they get to court, the dealers face lengthy stays in prison. However, none of those efforts will keep aerosol cans out of the hands of a fourteen-year-old huffer. That problem must be attacked in other ways.

First-Time Use Can Be Fatal

What is particularly troubling about inhalant abuse is that few young people realize just how dangerous the practice can be. Even a first-time user can suffer a fatal overdose, becoming a victim of sudden sniffing death syndrome. In addition, many young people do not realize that most inhalants are flammable and highly volatile, and that they risk their lives just by handling the chemicals. An errant spark or ember can easily cause serious injury or death. Suffocation through inhalant abuse is also common; young people who have wrapped plastic bags around their heads to enhance their highs have choked to death.

About a hundred deaths a year are attributed to inhalants, but that statistic may be understated. According to David Shurtleff, director of the Division of Basic Neuroscience and Behavioral Research for the National Institute on Drug Abuse, medical examiners are only beginning to test for evidence of inhalant abuse in the bodies of young victims. "People fear heroin and cocaine, but when you look at the prevalence rates of these drugs in kids and teens, it's relatively low compared to inhalants," Shurtleff said. "And the reason for that is availability."[2]

Chronic inhalant abusers lucky enough to avoid death face a host of physical, mental, and social problems. The chemicals in inhaled substances are known to destroy brain cells, impeding mental development and leaving users with long-lasting physical handicaps. Also, it has been proven that inhalant abusers lose interest in schoolwork. Their dropout rates are high. They may turn to crime and find themselves imprisoned.

Warning Young People About the Danger

Inhalants are often the first drug a young person will try. Before he or she sneaks that first cigarette, drinks that first beer, or experiments with that first marijuana joint, it is likely that the young person will seek a cheap and quick high by sniffing glue or huffing the nitrous oxide from a can of whipped cream. Such experimenting may begin when young people are in elementary school. "If you look at some of the data, first use on average is about twelve years of age,"[3] explains Harvey Weiss of the National Inhalant Prevention Coalition.

That is why the authors of a study on inhalant abuse published in the *Journal of the American Academy of Child and Adolescent Psychiatry* have urged educators to start explaining the dangers of inhalant abuse to young people in elementary school. The aim is to stop the early experimenting. "Delaying the age at first inhalant use may help reduce the risk of progressing to abuse or dependence,"[4] according to the authors.

Weiss said young people do listen. His group was founded in Texas in 1990 to run a statewide program. It obtained government funding to spread the word about inhalant abuse in Texas schools, offering programs to students as early as kindergarten age. Weiss said the statistics soon showed a decline in inhalant abuse by young people in Texas. But in 1995, budget cuts forced the state to end its support for anti-inhalant programs. "Within six or seven months, the next time a survey came around, inhalant use had skyrocketed," Weiss said. "There has to be a consistent message out there."[5]

Despite their urgent pleas, advocacy groups have often found themselves confronting some people that do not recognize the severity of the inhalant problem or the importance of handling it seriously. According to the National Inhalant Prevention Coali-

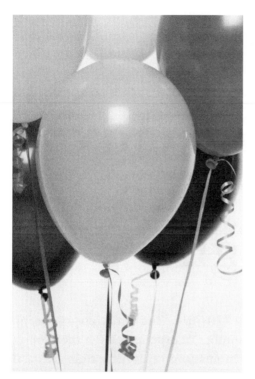 

Even seemingly harmless products like helium balloons or magic markers present a danger if abused by huffers or sniffers.

tion, such nationally known corporations as Toys "R" Us, FedEx, and McDonald's have aired commercials showing characters inhaling helium. In addition, trailers for the 2004 film *Scooby-Doo 2: Monsters Unleashed* included a scene showing a character inhaling nitrous oxide from a can of whipped cream. Protests ensued, and the scene was cut before the film was released. "Right now, there's barely any public awareness out there," Weiss said. "And in the young person's mind, how can they think this is dangerous if they're not told? They think it's just household stuff."[6]

Chapter 1

A Cheap and Easy Way to Get High

During the 1760s and 1770s, the English scientist Joseph Priestley conducted a number of experiments on the properties of air, using different combinations of oxygen, nitrogen, and other gases. Priestley was concerned about pollution and was looking to make air cleaner. He also searched for a method to purify air, so that fire could be made to burn hotter and longer. Priestley said he wanted to find "an air five or six times as good as common air."[7] His experiments led to many discoveries, one of which was carbonated water—the essential component of soda pop. Another of his major discoveries was nitrous oxide, although at the time even Priestley himself did not recognize the significance of the gas he had created by combining two parts of nitrogen with one part of oxygen. Priestley could not foresee the benefits of nitrous oxide, nor did he anticipate how its abuse would jeopardize people's lives.

Discovering Uses
In 1799, Humphry Davy, another English chemist, caught a whiff of nitrous oxide while searching for a painkiller to administer to patients undergoing surgery. Davy noticed that the vapors made

him giddy, and he told his friends about this new "wonder gas." Soon, nitrous oxide parties were quite popular among members of British society. The parties' hosts would pass around to their guests a bottle of liquid nitrous oxide, with the container uncorked so guests could inhale the vapors.

Many people enjoyed these nitrous oxide parties. Among devoted users of the gas were the poet Samuel Taylor Coleridge and the physician and scholar Peter Roget, author of *Roget's Thesaurus*. Coleridge, Roget, and the other happy members of British society who attended nitrous oxide parties were probably history's first huffers and sniffers.

Davy's experiments did eventually lead to a practical use for nitrous oxide. He recommended that it be employed as a painkiller for patients facing surgery. Although nitrous oxide would not be tested as a painkiller until 1845, when a dentist named Horace Wells tried it on a patient, the gas proved to be effective. By the 1860s dentists regularly used nitrous oxide, which was sometimes called "laughing gas."

The English chemist Humphry Davy helped to make nitrous oxide, or "laughing gas," popular in Britain.

Over the years, as medical researchers experimented with different painkilling methods, the vapors from other chemicals would also be employed to dull pain and put patients to sleep. For example, chloroform and ether surfaced as effective analgesics; eventually, however, both were discarded because of their serious side effects—liver and kidney damage, nausea, vomiting, and even sudden death among them. Laughing gas, though, did not appear to produce ill effects, so its use continued.

More than a century later, nitrous oxide continues to be used as a painkiller. As Dr. Steven Sullivan, an oral surgeon in Oklahoma, explained to a reporter, "Nitrous oxide allays feelings of apprehension and allows patients to become more calm and relaxed, thus reducing any stress associated with a trip to the dentist."[8] Because of this, nitrous oxide is still employed in dental offices and hospitals, albeit under tightly controlled conditions supervised by medical professionals trained in the administration of anesthetics.

A nineteenth-century dentist anesthetizes his patient using nitrous oxide. The gas, an effective painkiller, is still used for certain procedures.

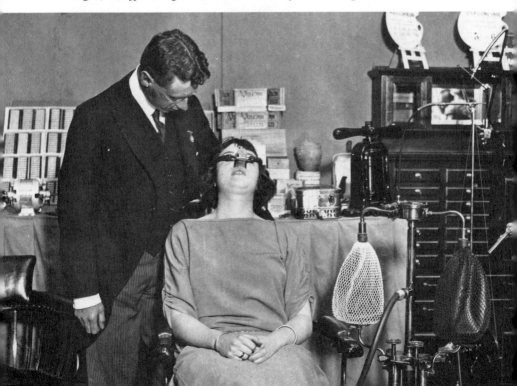

The medical establishment's long use of nitrous oxide for legitimate purposes does not mean the party crowd ever gave up on recreational use of the gas. Among the well-to-do during the latter half of the nineteenth century, nitrous oxide continued to be inhaled to brighten up a dull get-together. Additionally, people discovered what they regarded as far more serious uses for the gas: they believed it cleared their minds and made them think in new ways. One of nitrous oxide's earliest proponents was Benjamin Paul Blood, who had his first experience with the gas in a dentist's chair. Blood fancied himself a writer and philosopher, although most of his musings on the meaning of life were published as letters to the local newspapers in his hometown of Amsterdam, New York. After getting his first whiff of the gas in 1860, Blood claimed to have gained "a Revelation or insight"[9] into the problems of mankind. His pamphlet, *The Anaesthetic Revelation and the Gist of Philosophy*, and his book, *Pluriverse: An Essay in the Philosophy of Pluralism*, promoted the use of nitrous oxide and other inhalants, arguing that philosophers as far back as the ancient Greek Plato had been under the influence of mind-altering drugs when they developed their ideas.

By the end of the nineteenth century, nitrous oxide had earned a following among writers and philosophers. The American philosopher and psychologist William James, for example, was a devoted user of nitrous oxide, claiming it cleared his mind, helped improve his writing, and allowed him to see truths not evident while sober. In an 1882 essay, "Subjective Effects of Nitrous Oxide," James wrote:

> I have sheet after sheet of phrases dictated or written during the intoxication, which to the sober reader seem meaningless drivel, but which at the moment of transcribing were fused in the fire of infinite rationality. God and devil, good and evil, life and death, I and thou, sober and drunk, matter and form, black and white, quality and quantity, shiver of ecstasy and shudder of horror, vomiting and swallowing, inspiration and expiration, fate and reason, great and small, extent and intent, joke and earnest, tragic and comic, and fifty other contrasts figure in these pages in the same monotonous way. . . . The thought of mutual implication of the parts . . . produced a perfect delirium of theoretic rapture.[10]

The American psychologist and philosopher William James believed that inhaling nitrous oxide helped him think more clearly.

Chemical Products for Everyday Use

During the nineteenth century, America's Industrial Revolution required the development of chemicals as vital components of production and manufacturing. Degreasers and other solvents, cleaning agents, gases, paints, and other coatings were developed during this era. World War I and World War II further encouraged the development of chemicals intended for industrial use, as factories devoted production to armament manufacturing.

The twentieth century also saw an increase in products developed for the consumer. One such product was the aerosol spray can. Its origins date to 1837, when a French inventor named Antoine Perpigna developed a soda siphon that released carbonated beverages from a can through a valve. In 1899, the chemicals methyl and ethyl chloride were employed as propellants in aerosol cans. Still, aerosol cans did not immediately come into widespread use because the valves that regulated the gases did not work well. It took until 1927 for a valve to be perfected by a Norwegian inventor named Erik Rotheim.

Fluorocarbons in the form of liquefied gases were first employed as aerosol-can propellants during World War II, as part of a U.S.-government project to develop an insect repellent for servicemen stationed in the Tropics. After the war, inventor Robert Abplanal developed a simple crimp-on valve that made aerosol spray cans cheap to mass-produce. Manufacturers now found aerosol cans to be an ideal way to make household products available to consumers. With a simple motion of the finger, a desired amount of hair spray, paint, deodorant, and many other products could be released.

Airplane Glue

In the early 1950s, the development of plastics and injection molding led entrepreneurs in the United States and Europe to launch the plastic modeling industry. Scale-model kits that enabled young people to assemble replicas of cars, airplanes, and ships went on the market and were an immediate success. A modeler's glue employing the solvent toluene, which helped the glue dry faster, was placed on the market as well. A small tube of it, called "airplane glue" was made available in every hobby store in America for only a few cents.

The first indication that young people were using common consumer-type chemicals to get high surfaced in Denver, Colorado, in 1959. At that time, newspapers reported that teenagers

During the 1950s, young people discovered that they could get high by sniffing the fumes from tubes of modeling glue.

were smearing airplane glue on the palms of their hands, then cup-
ping their hands over their mouths and noses and inhaling deeply.
Parents were finding their glue-sniffing children dizzy and disori-
ented. One glue-sniffing teenager told *Time* magazine, "You take
a tube of plastic glue, the kind the squares use to make model airplanes, and you squeeze it all out in a handkerchief, see. . . . It's
simple and it's cheap. It's quick, too. Man!"[11]

By June 1960, Denver police said they had investigated some
fifty cases of glue sniffing. Even though at that point there had
never been a scientific study performed on the dangers of glue
sniffing, authorities suspected that nothing good would come of
the practice. One Denver police official told a newspaper reporter,
"I'm afraid some kid will get hold of too much of the stuff and
we'll have a fatal case on our hands."[12] That prediction would
prove to be remarkably accurate.

Narcotic Effect

The practice of sniffing glue was not confined to the Rocky
Mountains. In 1961, the *New York Times* reported that many
youths in suburban Long Island communities had turned to sniffing glue for the "narcotic effect." The newspaper reported: "Toxic
fumes from a chemical ingredient in a model airplane glue are
being inhaled by some youngsters to obtain a feeling of elation
similar to that of narcotics."[13]

By the end of 1962, New York City police had arrested nearly
eight hundred people for sniffing glue. In 1963, that number
jumped to more than two thousand. Still, public health officials
and social workers believed that the number of arrests should have
been even larger and that police actually were catching only a small
minority of glue-sniffing teenagers. New York City social worker
Robert Cooper told *Newsweek* magazine, "Of the 16,000 way-out
adolescents we come in contact with, I'd guess that fifteen percent were glue sniffing. It's on the increase."[14]

Police arrested people for sniffing glue, even though there were
no laws specifically forbidding the practice. (Often, glue sniffers
were charged with public drunkenness.) In 1963, the *New York*

Times reported that some retailers were actually selling airplane glue to youths along with plastic bags they could use to huff the fumes. The city's board of health soon responded to the practice, banning airplane glue sales to anyone under the age of eighteen.

Authorities first discovered that teenagers were sniffing something other than airplane glue when police in Salt Lake City, Utah, took a dozen glue sniffers into custody. During questioning, seven of them admitted that they regularly sniffed gasoline fumes. Other

Sniffing Gasoline

There is no inhalant more plentiful today than gasoline. It is found in every car parked on every street and driveway in every city and town in the United States. In addition, many people store gasoline in containers in their garages so they can power lawn mowers and other tools.

Because gasoline is so readily available, it is among the most abused inhalants. The U.S. Substance Abuse and Mental Health Services Administration reported in 2003 that 3 percent of all teenage inhalers admit to sniffing gasoline vapors, placing it second as an abused product, only slightly behind toluene, which is reportedly used by 3.6 percent of teenage inhalers. Gasoline and toluene are the most-abused inhalants because they are the most widely available.

An early study on inhaling gasoline was conducted in 1970 by Dr. Ewart A. Swinyard of the University of Utah College of Medicine. He reported that people who sniff gasoline often exhibit symptoms similar to people who drink too much alcohol. In a 1972 issue of *Consumer Reports* magazine, Swinyard explained, "The signs and symptoms include incoordination, restlessness, excitement, confusion, disorientation . . . and, finally, coma that may last for a few hours to several days."

Other short-term effects of sniffing gasoline include headaches, blurred vision, nausea, vertigo, ringing in the ears, and loss of appetite. Over the long term, chronic inhalers of gasoline fumes can develop leukemia, the cancer that attacks the bone marrow.

Swinyard also found that people who sniff gasoline fumes can become giddy and dizzy. They often hallucinate. The *Consumer Reports* article cited a 1955 interview that Massachusetts educator A.E. Hamilton conducted with a boy nicknamed "Bullet," who related his experiences sniffing gasoline fumes. In the interview, Bullet talked of hallucinating. He said, "If you have a lot it makes you sort of dream. It gets all dark and you see shooting stars in it, and this time I saw big flies flying in it. They were big and green and had white wings."

Buzz Bomb, Boppers, and Bolt

Inhalant abusers employ numerous street terms to describe their habits as well as the substances they inhale. Bagging, for example, means to inhale substances that have been sprayed into a plastic or paper bag. Similarly, ballooning is inhaling gases that have been injected into a balloon. Bagging and ballooning are done by people who abuse whippets. These abusers first empty the whippets into bags or balloons because the nitrous oxide they contain is very cold. If abusers were to inhale the gas directly out of the whippet, they could suffer frostbite to their lips, mouths, and even internal organs.

Nitrous oxide is known as buzz bomb on the streets. Using nitrous oxide is often called shooting the breeze. Amyl nitrite, a prescription drug inhaled to relieve heart pain that has found its way onto the illegal market, is known by abusers as ames, pearls, boppers, and poppers because the small glass vial that holds the drug makes a "pop" when the user breaks it open.

A gluey is a user who sniffs glue. Butyl nitrite has several nicknames, including thrust, snapper, rush, hardware, and bolt. Some general street terms for inhalants are medusa, moon gas, kick, hippie crack, huff, oz, bullet, bang, poor man's pot, and air blast.

new information came from an incident in Washington, D.C. A music teacher there told *Time* magazine that one of her students—who had previously refused to sing a single note—came to class one day with permanent markers, which he uncapped and sniffed behind his songbook. Suddenly, the teacher said, "He got up and sang like a bird."[15]

As cases of inhalant abuse spread throughout the country, medical researchers started looking into its effects. A 1962 study published in the *Journal of the American Medical Association* concluded that inhaling the fumes from airplane glue "may cause damage to the liver, kidneys and brain."[16] State legislatures reacted swiftly, making glue sniffing a crime, but young people continued to turn to airplane glue in search of a quick and cheap high.

It took manufacturers of airplane glue until the late 1960s to find a way to make their products less appealing to sniffers. At that point, they found that adding mustard seed oil to the mix produced tearing and gagging in abusers, so they added it to deter abuse. Nonetheless, even today, some household glues that contain toluene as well as other solvents continue to be abused.

New Ways to Get High

By the early 1970s, young people found a new way to get high from consumer products: inhaling the gases in aerosol cans. In 1971, the U.S. Food and Drug Administration reported that more than a hundred young people had died from heart attacks since 1967 as a result of inhaling aerosol fluorocarbons; usually, the FDA said, the victims would inflate plastic bags or balloons with the products, then inhale the gases. "Once the final event begins, it's quick, sudden, and irreversible,"[17] Dr. Rita Bass of the Connecticut Department of Mental Health told a news reporter.

Aerosol industry leaders agreed to attach warning labels to their products, admonishing users to "avoid excessive inhalation, which

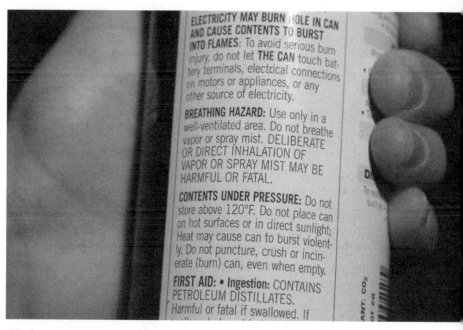

Under pressure from antidrug activists, in the 1970s manufacturers began placing labels on the backs of aerosol cans, warning about the danger of inhaling fumes.

Inexpensive, disposable cigarette lighters provided another way for inhalant abusers to get high.

may be harmful," but members of Congress did not think young people searching for a quick high would pay much attention to the labels. "Even with warning labels, I doubt that a high percentage of users are aware of the hazards,"[18] said Pennsylvania congressman Fred B. Rooney.

Meanwhile, American industry was developing new products for consumers—and some of these products, it turned out, could be abused by huffers and sniffers. In 1973, for example, the first mass-produced butane cigarette lighters arrived in American stores. Butane gas had been employed in cigarette lighters as early as 1933, but the lighters were expensive and therefore not popular with most smokers. In the 1950s, attempts were made to mass-market butane lighters in the United States, but the business was abandoned because the manufacturers still were unable to produce and market the lighters at a price most consumers were willing to pay. Also problematic was the fact that the mechanical apparatus that sparked the flame in early butane lighters often failed to work.

Finally, by the 1970s, the technical problems were solved, and a small, disposable butane lighter costing less than a dollar became available. Consumers found them easy to use; the lighters no longer had to have their smelly and messy liquid lighter fluid refilled. Instead, when the fluid was used up, the lighters were simply tossed away, because they could be replaced at such a low price. With so many advantages, butane lighters became immensely popular. Millions were sold. Unfortunately, it did not take long for sniffers to figure out they could get high by inhaling the butane out of the lighter's top.

An International Problem

Inhalant abuse is not just a problem in the United States. Around the globe, millions of young people as well as adults have discovered what many American teenagers already know: common household products can provide a cheap and quick high. Health officials in countries as diverse as Japan, Nigeria, Hungary, and Great Britain have recognized inhalants as a threat to the lives of their citizens.

This abuse is particularly widespread in Central and South America. Bolivia, Brazil, Peru, Colombia, Mexico, and other Latin American countries have large populations of impoverished young people who get high with inhalants to escape the bleak realities of living on the streets. There are some 50 million "street kids" in Latin American countries, and a "huge percentage" of them have turned to inhalant abuse, Dr. Neil Rosenberger, a professor of medicine at the University of Colorado and founder of the International Institute on Inhalant Abuse, said in a 2003 interview with the *Honolulu Star-Bulletin*. "Guys who sell glue make a good living. They steal a big tub of glue and dole it out in baby food jars."

In Brazil, more than 40 percent of the population is composed of people under the age of eighteen. In a 1995 National Institute on Drug Abuse study, editors Nicholas Kozel, Zili Sloboda, and Mario De La Rose wrote: "Given that the major drug abuse problem for young people is the use of inhalants, this behavior presents a particular challenge for Brazil. In some geographic areas, inhalant abuse among youths with other problems is concentrated in poverty areas. In times of economic hardship, these children end up in the streets and become involved in the use of alcohol and in petty crime." Meanwhile, in Mexico and Peru, inhalants rank third in substances abused by young people, trailing only alcohol and tobacco. In Peru, the study authors reported, "Among marginalized children, inhalant use and abuse is high, with the majority of these children reporting that they use inhalants on a daily basis."

Huffing and sniffing are international problems. These two Honduran teens, high on glue, are among millions of young people worldwide who abuse inhalants.

Butane sniffers faced perils besides damage to their lungs and other internal organs. Because butane is highly flammable, some sniffers found themselves catching on fire while trying to enjoy their highs. A recent case reported in Great Britain told of four young butane sniffers hospitalized after the butane they were inhaling in a garage caught fire and caused an explosion. "Apparently, the four—three boys and a girl—had been sniffing butane in [a] parent's car, inside the garage," a Warrington, England, fire service spokesman told a reporter. "After they had finished, one of them struck a match to light a cigarette and there was a terrific explosion. They are incredibly lucky to have escaped alive. Fortunately, the garage roof was of a flimsy structure, allowing the blast to escape mainly upwards."[19]

Potentially Dangerous Products

Another consumer product that quickly became popular was liquid correction fluid. Today, most people type on computer terminals, and corrections can be done right on the screen before a printout is made. Yet before personal computers were available, most people used typewriters to create documents or fill out forms. Correcting mistakes on a typewriter is not as easy as deleting a misspelling on a personal computer; erasing might smear the line and ruin the entire page. To make the process easier, during the 1980s a solvent-based correction fluid was developed. A typist spotting an error on a page simply had to dab a little white paint on the mistake, wait a short time, then type the correct character over the spot that had been "whited out." The tiny bottle even came with a brush affixed to the cap. Millions of bottles were sold to office workers throughout the United States. However, because correction fluid contains toluene—the same solvent used in airplane glue—a new product was suddenly available to the inhalant abuser.

As other new consumer products were developed, inhalant users constantly found ways to get high from them. For example, videocassette recorders went on the market in the 1980s; to keep the recording heads clean, manufacturers sold home cleaning kits

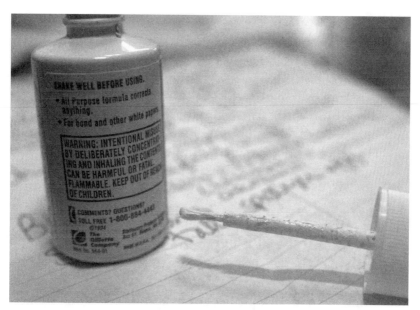

Like airplane glue, liquid correction fluid contains toluene. This chemical produces the high, but also makes the fumes dangerous to inhale.

that employed butyl nitrite, a commonly abused chemical. And once desktop computers replaced typewriters, the expensive and complicated machines had to be maintained. Suddenly, there was a market for cleaners to keep the keyboards, disk drives, and other electronic components running smoothly. Most computer cleaning fluids contain dimethyl ether, a derivative of the unstable chemical previously employed as a painkiller before doctors discovered how dangerous ether could be.

Additionally, new uses have been found for nitrous oxide, the great-grandfather of abused inhalants. Today, nitrous oxide is used in cans of whipped cream as a propellant. When the can is turned upside down and the nozzle is triggered at a dish of pumpkin pie, for example, the nitrous oxide causes the cream to expand and come out whipped and fluffy. Meanwhile, the gas dissolves in the cream. Some inhalant abusers try to coax gas out of the cans without releasing the cream. Others have discovered an even more readily available source of the gas—the tiny canisters used to charge whipped cream cans. These canisters, called "whippets," are available in some grocery stores, in dairies, and on the Internet. They come in cartons of twelve and twenty-four, and cost about two dollars each.

People who own high-performance cars have found that injecting nitrous oxide into their carburetors makes their vehicles faster. Automotive supply distributors sell nitrous oxide in bulk quantities. However, to discourage huffing, manufacturers now add hydrogen sulfide to the gas. This gives the nitrous fumes an unpleasant smell.

Irreversible Damage

Over the past few decades, human services agencies, schools, and advocacy groups have issued warnings and tried to educate young people about the dangers of sniffing and huffing, but inhalant abuse among young people has continued. There is no question that the overwhelming availability of consumer products that con-

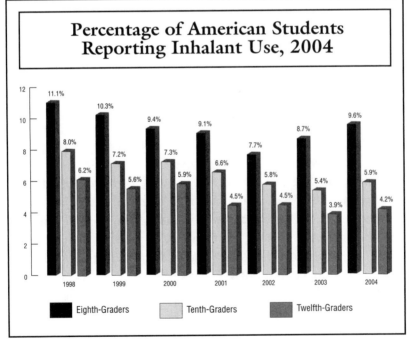

Percentage of American Students Reporting Inhalant Use, 2004

Eighth-Graders   Tenth-Graders   Twelfth-Graders

Source: 2004 *Monitoring the Future* study

tain mind-altering substances—it is believed that more than fourteen hundred are on the market—has made it difficult to keep these products out of the hands of young abusers.

There is no greater evidence of that fact than a study released in 2003 by the U.S. Substance Abuse and Mental Health Services Administration (SAMHSA), which estimated that some 23 million Americans over the age of twelve have tried inhalants at least once in their lifetimes. That number represents nearly 10 percent of all Americans over the age of twelve.

Another set of troubling statistics regarding inhalant use by young people was included in the University of Michigan's annual *Monitoring the Future* study of drug abuse. Released in late 2004, the study found that inhalant use is on the rise among students in the eighth, tenth, and twelfth grades. Eighth-grade students showed the sharpest increase. The study reported that nearly 10 percent of all eighth-grade students had tried inhalants during 2004, which represented a rise of almost 1 percent over numbers recorded in 2003. The rise in use among tenth- and twelfth-grade students was more modest, yet nearly 6 percent of all tenth-graders and more than 4 percent of all twelfth-grade students reported using inhalants in 2004. The *Monitoring the Future* study reported those numbers at the same time it reported that among young people, use of other drugs, such as marijuana, heroin, and cocaine, had declined in 2004.

The authors of the *Monitoring the Future* report wrote, "Use of inhalants has consistently been highest among eighth-graders, likely because these products are inexpensive, legal, and easy to obtain, making them more attractive to younger adolescents who have less access to illicit drugs."[20]

The study pointed out that inhalant abuse had been showing a gradual decline since 1995, due mostly to the efforts of antidrug organizations, such as the Partnership for a Drug-Free America, whose programs call attention to the dangers of inhalant abuse. However, the *Monitoring the Future* authors remarked, "Use by eighth-graders increased significantly . . . and the investigators called attention to the fact that the use of this class of drugs may be about to rebound. This year, inhalant use continued to increase among eighth-graders, and for the first time in recent years increased in the upper two grades as well."[21]

The *Monitoring the Future* study also found that among students in the eighth and tenth grades, there was a decline in the percentage who believe using inhalants is risky behavior. This decline came at the same time *Monitoring the Future* reported an increase in the number of young people who believe drugs like nicotine and marijuana could be dangerous to their health. According to Lloyd Johnston, the principal *Monitoring the Future* investigator:

> The proportion of young people who believe it is dangerous to use inhalants has declined among both eighth- and tenth-graders over the past three years, which quite possibly explains the rebound in use. This turnaround in their use continues to suggest the need for greater attention to the dangers of inhalant use in our media messages and in-school prevention programs.[22]

The statistics reported in the *Monitoring the Future* study certainly spell out the extent of the problem of inhalant abuse in the United States, but they do not tell the full story of what awaits the young person who inhales toxic fumes to get high. People who huff or sniff chemicals risk damage to their bodies and brains that is often irreversible. Beyond that, some inhalant abusers, seeking nothing more than a cheap and quick high, may unexpectedly suffer the ultimate consequence—death.

Chapter 2

The Physical Effects of Inhalants

Those inhaling dangerous substances face a long list of physical and psychological risks the moment they take their first huffs. In seeking a high that often lasts no more than a few seconds, they may suffer permanent brain damage that can leave them unable to form even simple sentences. They may also suffer physical ailments that range from paralysis to poor eyesight and hearing loss. Some inhalant abusers contract cancer because the chemicals they ingest are highly carcinogenic. Pregnant women who abuse inhalants put their babies at risk. Worst of all, many inhalant abusers lose their lives, falling victim to a condition known as sudden sniffing death syndrome, which affects both chronic abusers and first-time huffers. Without warning, even a seemingly modest inhalation from an aerosol can or a butane lighter can be fatal.

Damaged Brain Cells

When people sniff gasoline vapors, fill a plastic bag with spray paint and inhale the fumes, or suck in nitrous oxide from whippets, they usually experience brief and sudden feelings of euphoria. Often, huffers and sniffers feel giddy and dizzy. Their speech may become slurred, and they may have difficulty walking. Some

Inhalants can cause serious psychological alterations. Certain products can even make a person senseless and unable to function.

inhalant abusers also have reported experiencing brief hallucinations.

In recent years, many researchers have concluded that inhalants affect the brain in much the same way as drugs like heroin, LSD, and marijuana. Inhalants do not seem to be physically addictive: unlike heroin and nicotine, for example, inhalants do not cause their users' bodies to crave the dangerous substances. Nevertheless, inhalants are psychologically addictive; abusers seek repeated doses, anxious to achieve their next highs. These abusers bodies' also build a resistance to the chemical, so they must take larger and more frequent doses to get high.

Inhalants alter the neurotransmitters in the brain. These are natural chemicals that carry messages from one brain cell to another. Sometimes, inhalants cause the brain cells to produce too many neurotransmitters, thus overwhelming the brain with information. This disruption in the flow of information among brain cells causes the temporary feelings of euphoria, giddiness, and dizziness in the inhalant user.

Additionally, inhalants affect the brain cells, or neurons, themselves. While healthy neurons are protected by a coating of fatty tissue known as myelin, the chemicals in inhalant vapors may become lodged in the myelin and break it down, slowing or even preventing neurons from transmitting messages.

Long-Term, Permanent Damage

The euphoria, giddiness, and dizziness may be temporary, but other effects from inhalant abuse are often long-term, permanent, and destructive. More specifically, when the brain cell's myelin breaks down completely, the cell is damaged. And when the neurotransmitter chemicals are slowed down or stopped, the wrong messages are usually delivered. For example, when an inhalant user's speech is slurred, his or her brain is telling the mouth to speak, but the chemicals from the inhalant are affecting the neurotransmitters and clouding their message. Therefore, the person's mouth is unable to form the words the brain instructs it to use. When enough brain cells are destroyed, slurred speech may become a permanent condition.

In the case of toluene, a common component of airplane glue and other products, the chemical alters the brain's ability to release the neurotransmitter known as dopamine, which enables the body to move and also regulates emotions, particularly the feeling of pleasure. By exposing their brain cells to toluene, glue sniffers often increase the amount of dopamine that travels from neuron to neuron. When too much dopamine is released, the brain compensates by reducing the number of dopamine receptors. Even so, if too much dopamine is suddenly released before the receptors have been reduced, the sudden surge is absorbed by the brain and causes the glue sniffer's mood swings as well as stumbling and lack of coordination. Also, because toluene is stimulating the brain to create dopamine, the body may make less dopamine on its own. This means that heavy glue sniffers may find it hard to feel happy during the periods when they are not under the influence of toluene.

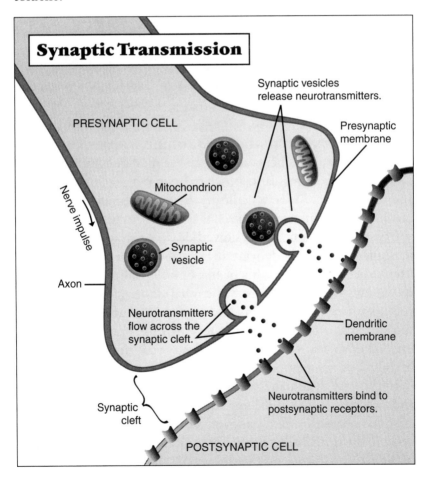

A Cocainelike High

Inhalants may provide a high similar to the euphoric feeling experienced by cocaine users. A study by the U.S. Department of Energy's Brookhaven National Laboratory in New York found that toluene mimics cocaine in how the drug stimulates the pleasure centers of the brain. Scientists at Brookhaven injected baboons with toluene, then performed brain scans on the animals to see what parts of their brains were affected. The scans showed the toluene headed directly for the brain cells that produce dopamine, the neurotransmitter that carries messages of pleasure.

"We have known it from behavioral studies—people will report euphoria and they will report highs," Stephen Dewey, a neuroanatomist at Brookhaven, told Maggie Fox of the Reuters news agency on April 16, 2002. "But we have never known this class of chemicals, these toluenes, go to the dopamine centers of the brain, much like cocaine."

Dewey said he decided to initiate the study because he does much lecturing to elementary school students on the dangers of drug abuse. During his lectures, Dewey said, he constantly fields questions from students about inhalant abuse.

It is believed that 60 percent of the chemicals from an inhalant make it into the user's bloodstream. The blood flows through the brain, where the chemicals do their damage to the neurons. The chemically tainted blood also flows through the heart, kidneys, liver, and lungs. Those organs are damaged as well.

Because the inhaler ingests substances by drawing in a breath, it is the lungs that get the first and fullest hit of the chemical. For example, people who abuse inhalants often find themselves suffering from shortness of breath. This may cause them to wheeze and cough. Because the lungs are not putting enough oxygen into the inhalant abuser's blood, a huffer's skin may develop a condition known as cyanosis, which turns the skin a shade of blue. Speaking about spray-paint sniffers, Jack Reyes, an associate professor of pediatrics at the University of Oklahoma Health Sciences Center, told a reporter, "People who sniff have a number of misconceptions about their addiction. Some may think that, since they inhale air and exhale air, they will exhale the paint. But that's not true. . . . These toxic compounds are going directly to the target organs, and the lungs get it first. The lungs, long-term, could be heavily damaged."[23]

Usually, the high provided by an inhalant will last only for a few seconds to a few minutes. One of the reasons the effects end so quickly is that the huffer or sniffer usually loses focus during the experience. To continue feeling high, the abuser must continue sniffing fumes. Yet once the initial jolt hits, the user often forgets to hold the source of the inhalant up to the nose or mouth, which breaks off the user's connection to the intoxicant. "As the user begins to experience a depressed state of consciousness, the user's hand falls away from the face, terminating exposure,"[24] says Dr. Milton Tenenbein, a physician and longtime expert on inhalant abuse who has written for the *Psychiatric Times*. This requirement to physically participate in the act of getting high makes using inhalants different from, for example, taking a dose of heroin or LSD. Heroin is injected into the body through an intravenous needle and, once the drug is injected, users need do nothing else but allow themselves to succumb to the high. Similarly, LSD is taken orally and requires no other action to maintain a high.

Risking Death Every Time

Of course, once inhalant abusers gather their wits about them, they can give themselves another jolt and then another and another—for as long as the butane, gasoline, or nitrous oxide holds out. Some young people prefer to get high that way. Others spread out their abuse of inhalants throughout the day, taking a hit here or there whenever they feel the urge. Yet regardless of whether they are binge inhalers or sporadic huffers and sniffers, young people who use inhalants risk death every time they put a gasoline-soaked rag to their nose or inhale the fumes from a butane lighter or other device or substance.

In one such instance, Freddy Bustaque, a sixteen-year-old Pennsylvania teenager, was late for a summer job. His father, Al Bustaque, believed his son had overslept. "Freddy, wake up. You're late,"[25] Al called at Freddy's bedroom door. When Freddy did not respond, his father cracked open the door. Freddy was

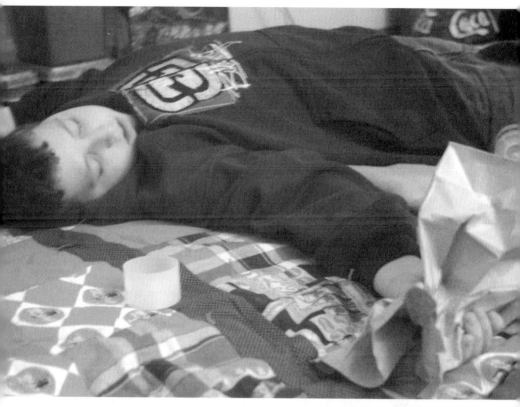

Young people who use inhalants are at risk for sudden sniffing death syndrome. In such cases, the high leads to cardiac arrest, which kills the user.

lying face up, sprawled across his bed and still clothed in what he had been wearing the previous night. Al Bustaque attempted to wake his son, then pulled away in horror when he realized the boy was lifeless. The father tried to administer mouth-to-mouth resuscitation, but he was far too late because Freddy had died overnight. An autopsy revealed that the toxic chemicals from a can of air freshener found near Freddy's bed had caused the boy's heart to stop.

Freddy's death illustrates just how deadly inhalants can be. It is likely that the teenager died from sudden sniffing death syndrome. Those who have researched the syndrome have concluded that a strong dose of an abused inhalant increases the sensitivity of the heart to adrenaline, a hormone released by the adrenal gland during times of emotional stress. A rush of adrenaline stimulates the heart and central nervous system, making muscles contract and blood pressure increase. Many athletes believe they perform better under stress because such an adrenaline rush makes their bodies stronger and faster. However, athletes are, of course, in top physical condition and have strong hearts, unlike the typical inhalant abuser. When the abuser becomes excited or frightened— typical reactions to an inhalant high—large quantities of adrenaline are released. In response, the abuser's heart, which also has been made weaker by the inhalant, beats wildly and erratically, sometimes leading to cardiac arrest. Sudden sniffing death syndrome can kill even a strong, otherwise healthy teenager. In-

Mixing Prescription Drugs with Inhalants

Teenagers who take prescription drugs subject themselves to added risks if they inhale dangerous substances. For example, young people who suffer from attention deficit disorder (ADD) often take the prescription drug Ritalin. This drug is a stimulant and causes the body to release adrenaline, which helps the ADD patient stay alert and focused. A sudden rush of adrenaline, however, can strain a person's heart. Teenagers who inhale solvents or other products while taking Ritalin or a similar stimulant experience a very strong adrenaline rush. Often these teenagers succumb to sudden sniffing death syndrome.

In 2004, officials in Ohio issued a warning to public health professionals, advising them of the risks that Ritalin patients face when they use inhalants, particularly substances that contain toluene, because of its damaging effects on the heart. Typewriter correction fluid was singled out as a product of concern. Earl Siegel, director of the drug and poison information center at Cincinnati Children's Hospital, said in an alert issued in 2004 by the Ohio Department of Alcohol and Drug Addictions Services, "I would be primarily and most concerned about a potential fatal interaction [whereby] the Ritalin having [an] adrenaline-like effect could enhance the possibility of Sudden Sniffing Death in the individual huffing correction fluid."

deed, it can kill any user of inhalants, even a first-time or occasional user.

Such an occurrence involved fifteen-year-old Jennifer Jones of Palm Beach Gardens, Florida, an honor student who dreamed of becoming an actress. In 1994, a friend urged Jennifer to try huffing. Four days later, she tried it again. This time, police found Jennifer's body under an air-conditioning unit in the family home. She had been huffing the refrigeration chemical from the air conditioner, and the substance had slowed her heart's ability to pump blood to her brain. Ironically, Jennifer's friend had convinced her that huffing was not as dangerous as taking illegal drugs and that all she would experience would be a brief period of light-headedness. "She told other kids that drugs would mess up their lives and that they shouldn't do them,"[26] Jennifer's mother, Grace Jones, told a reporter.

Other Inhalant Deaths

Sometimes, inhaling causes death, but not right away. Brad Kaye, a fifteen-year-old boy from Oklahoma, was the type of inhalant abuser who liked to take multiple hits at a time. One day in April 1992, Brad and his friends went on a butane-huffing binge. Each boy inhaled butane as much as twenty times in the space of a few minutes. Brad was still holding the can of butane when he collapsed in his friend's yard. His heart and lungs failed, and his kidneys shut down. By the time an ambulance got Brad to a nearby hospital, his brain was showing no activity. "I see a couple of these a year and they're always fatal," a doctor told Brad's horrified parents. Indeed, the doctor said that if Brad did emerge from his coma, he would probably be in a vegetative state. "He was without oxygen for too long,"[27] the doctor said. Brad Kaye never awoke from his coma and died the next day.

There are other ways to die from huffing and sniffing aside from suffering sudden sniffing death syndrome or otherwise falling victim to the toxic qualities of the chemicals. For instance, huffers who fill plastic bags with the fumes from spray-paint cans, then place the bags over their heads, can suffocate. Also, they can drown in their own vomit if the inhalants make them sick and unconscious. "If the user passes out, the bag can collapse and cover both the nose and the mouth," writes Dr. Milton Tenenbein. "Death due to dangerous behavior is a consequence of the . . . poor judgment while under the influence of inhalants with death resulting from falls, fires and drownings."[28]

Some inhalant users do not die from the physiological effects of the chemicals, but as a result of what happens when the highly flammable fumes come into contact with a spark or a lit match. In one such case in 1992, sixteen-year-old Michael Rubin died from severe burns suffered when a furnace exploded. Investigators suspected that the New Jersey teenager had been inhaling propane when the highly flammable gas was touched off by the pilot light in the nearby furnace.

Additionally, those under the influence of inhalants may attempt to drive a car, lose control of it, and become seriously injured or die in an accident. One of the most horrific examples occurred in 1999, when five juniors from Penncrest High School in Pennsylvania died after their car crashed into a tree. A medical examiner's report stated that the driver and three other girls in the car had been under the influence of difluoroethane, a component of a product used to clean computer keyboards. Dr. Dimitrie L. Contostavlos, the medical examiner, concluded that "driver impairment, with the loss of control on a straight road in daylight, in good weather, with no other traffic involved, resulted not from youthful inexperience and a dangerous stretch of road, but primarily from intoxication due to inhalation abuse."[29]

No Place Behind the Wheel

A year after the high schoolers' fatal accident in Pennsylvania, a conference sponsored by the U.S. National Highway Traffic Safety Administration examined issues surrounding drug abuse and driving. The conference was attended by toxicologists—scientists who study the effect of chemicals and other substances on the human body. The toxicologists studied sixteen drugs and similar substances, including some that are legally available as over-the-counter medications as well as drugs available only through pre-scriptions. Also, several illegal drugs—including cocaine, mari-juana, and LSD—were studied. The toxicologists' goal was to determine whether people under the influence of those drugs could safely operate motor vehicles.

One of the substances the toxicologists studied was toluene. They reached the conclusion that people inhaling this substance have no place behind the wheel of a car. The toxicologists looked at the arrest and hospital records in a total

A man visits a memorial to the Pennsylvania girls killed in a 1999 car accident. The girls had been inhaling fumes from a commercial spray duster (inset) just before the crash.

The Damage Inhalants Can Do to the Body and Brain

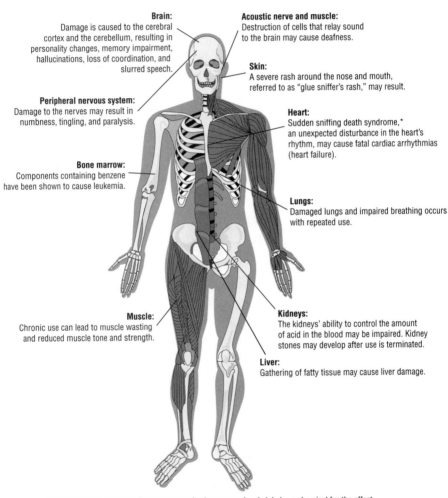

Brain:
Damage is caused to the cerebral cortex and the cerebellum, resulting in personality changes, memory impairment, hallucinations, loss of coordination, and slurred speech.

Peripheral nervous system:
Damage to the nerves may result in numbness, tingling, and paralysis.

Bone marrow:
Components containing benzene have been shown to cause leukemia.

Muscle:
Chronic use can lead to muscle wasting and reduced muscle tone and strength.

Acoustic nerve and muscle:
Destruction of cells that relay sound to the brain may cause deafness.

Skin:
A severe rash around the nose and mouth, referred to as "glue sniffer's rash," may result.

Heart:
Sudden sniffing death syndrome,* an unexpected disturbance in the heart's rhythm, may cause fatal cardiac arrhythmias (heart failure).

Lungs:
Damaged lungs and impaired breathing occurs with repeated use.

Kidneys:
The kidneys' ability to control the amount of acid in the blood may be impaired. Kidney stones may develop after use is terminated.

Liver:
Gathering of fatty tissue may cause liver damage.

*Sudden sniffing death syndrome may result when a user deeply inhales a chemical for the effect of intoxication. This causes a decrease in available oxygen in the body. If the user becomes startled or engages in sudden physical activity, an increased flow of adrenaline from the brain to the heart induces cardiac arrest and death occurs within minutes.

of one hundred and thirty-six cases involving toluene abusers who had been driving erratically and were taken into custody by police. Typically, the scientists' report stated, the symptoms exhibited by the sniffers included "dizziness, euphoria, grandiosity, floating sensation, drowsiness, reduced ability to concentrate, slowed reaction time, distorted perception of time and distance, confusion, weakness, fatigue, memory loss, delusions, and hallucinations." The scientists concluded: "Acute and chronic exposure to toluene can result in severe impairment."[30]

Other evidence suggests toluene is not the only inhalant that can impair judgment, slow reaction time, and affect a driver's ability to concentrate. In late 2004, inhalant abuse was suspected to be a factor in a fatal car accident in Sacramento County, California. The accident occurred in the early hours of the morning as a group of teen boys returned from celebrating a birthday. According to police, the teens' car jumped a curb, then traveled another seven hundred and seventy feet before crashing into a concrete wall. Police estimated that at the moment of collision, the car was traveling ninety miles per hour. One boy, fifteen-year-old Matthew Walas, was killed in the crash; two others were critically injured and died a few weeks later.

A coroner's report determined that Walas had traces of difluoroethane in his body at the time of his death. Matthew's mother, Sharon Walas, told a reporter, "I want kids to know this happened, that these kids were inhaling and it may have had something to do with the accident. I guess they call this 'huffing.' I never even knew what it was until a police officer explained it to me after the accident."[31]

Short-Term Effects

Inhalant abusers who are fortunate enough to avoid a fatal accident or sudden sniffing death syndrome still face dangers. Repeated huffing and sniffing can lead to a host of physical and mental problems that can affect abusers for the rest of their lives. Short-term effects can be highly unpleasant as well. Immediate effects include red spots and sores around the nose and mouth (where the caustic chemicals inhalers abuse come into contact with their skin), red and runny eyes and noses, a drunken and dazed aftermath of the high, nausea, and loss of appetite. Also, many users suffer painful headaches immediately after huffing and sniffing. Additionally, the inhaler may suffer frostbite around the mouth, nose, tongue, and throat, because the chemicals inhalers abuse are sometimes very cold when released from their containers.

Aside from these physical effects, huffers and sniffers face short-term mental and emotional consequences, some of which can be quite severe. Specifically, inhalant abusers may find themselves anxious, excitable, and irritable. Typically, many do poorly in school because they suffer from short-term memory loss. For example, Brad Kaye, who abused inhalants for more than a year before his death, had always been a good student. But in the final few months before his fatal dose of butane, Brad started failing tests. "I don't know what's wrong with me," he told his mother. "I just can't remember anything anymore."[32]

Long-Term and Permanent Damage

Inhalants may also cause the user's eyesight to deteriorate, and his or her muscle tone to erode. Moreover, inhalant abuse may affect the nervous system: repeated exposure to heavy doses of nitrous oxide has caused nerve damage in some people, resulting in permanent feelings of numbness in fingers and toes. Nitrous oxide also can leave female abusers sterile. This gas also depresses the central nervous system, sometimes to the point where breathing stops; after a few minutes, brain damage results. In the case of toluene, inhalation of its fumes can lead to hearing loss.

Dr. Tenenbein has been treating inhalant abusers for several years at Children's Hospital in Winnipeg, Canada. He regularly sees patients who have lost their hearing from sniffing glue that contains toluene. In some cases, young patients arrive at the hospital in some degree of paralysis—they have lost the ability to use arms or legs due to a condition known as peripheral neuropathy. Tenenbein reported that some of his paralyzed patients used inhalants for as few as six months. He has found that with treatment and therapy, most patients can learn to use their arms and legs again. Yet, Tenenbein said, patients who suffer brain damage are likely to never regain their full mental faculties.

In some cases, a patient may be left with almost no memory. For example, at the Colorado Mental Health Institute in Pueblo, social worker Lana Leonard told a news reporter about a patient named Joe, whose mother became concerned after her son started exhibiting erratic and violent behavior. The woman took her son to a doctor, who diagnosed Joe with brain damage caused by inhalant abuse. Once a popular boy and good athlete, Joe has since found he has trouble communicating with others—even though at one point he was fluent in both English and Spanish. In an article titled "Is Your Child Huffing?" Leonard explained to reporter Anita Bartholomew that Joe has almost no memory—too many of his brain cells were destroyed.

In addition to the emotional distress caused by inhalant abuse, young users may experience memory loss, nerve damage, and hearing loss.

"Are you feeling chilly today?" Leonard asked Joe, who responded, "Air is orangey."[33] As Leonard explained, that was Joe's way of telling her he was cold, because he was unable to find the right words to explain his feeling.

"How old are you?" Leonard asked. Joe slowly held up three fingers and mumbled, "Three."[34]

Leonard said Joe had abused inhalants as a teenager. Joe was thirty-two years old at the time of Leonard's interview with the reporter, and Joe had been under the care of the hospital in Pueblo for six years.

Some of the long-term consequences stemming from inhalant abuse—slow cognitive development, memory loss, and slurred speech, for example—are readily observed. Other damage is harder to see. Many chemicals favored by sniffers and huffers are carcinogenic, meaning they cause cancer. For example, repeated exposure to benzene, a component of gasoline, can cause leukemia, which is the cancer that attacks bone marrow.

Other complications of inhalant abuse include hepatitis, jaundice, emotional instability, staggering and stumbling, a loss of the sense of smell, and the condition known as nystagmus, which is an involuntary fluttering of the eyeballs.

Fetal Solvent Syndrome

Pregnant women who use inhalants not only place themselves at risk, but in most cases also do damage to their unborn babies. The same effects suffered by teenagers and adults—the wearing away of the myelin layer; the destruction of brain cells; the impact on the heart, lungs, liver, and other organs—is also suffered by the unborn baby growing inside the mother. Because the unborn fetus is still developing physically, these effects can be particularly damaging.

When a pregnant woman huffs or sniffs, her baby may become afflicted with a condition known as fetal solvent syndrome. The condition is similar to fetal alcohol syndrome, which affects the babies born to women who drink significant amounts of alcohol during their pregnancies. The signs and symptoms of fetal solvent

Nitrous Oxide and Pregnancy

Repeated exposure to nitrous oxide may impair a woman's ability to conceive, according to a study performed by the National Institute of Environmental Health Sciences. Teenage girls considering inhaling nitrous oxide whippets should certainly bear that fact in mind, but the findings of the study are even more troubling for female dental assistants, whose work often brings them into contact with nitrous oxide.

The study, reported in the October 3, 1992, edition of *Science News,* found that dental assistants exposed to high levels of nitrous oxide were only 41 percent as likely to conceive babies as dental employees who had less exposure to the gas. The exact role nitrous oxide plays in preventing conception is unknown, although the gas may impede development of a fertilized egg.

The American Dental Association has long urged its members to minimize employees' exposure to nitrous oxide. Many dentists employ equipment that vents unused or exhaled gas away from the examination room. "It makes sense not to expose staff and dentists to an agent that poses a concern in this way," said Patricia A. Baird, a University of British Columbia researcher who also has studied the effect of nitrous oxide on pregnancy and who was quoted in *Science News.*

In addition to dental office employees, other workers must be wary of inhaling stray chemical fumes in their workplaces. These workers include physicians, nurses, shoemakers, hair stylists, painters, and dry-cleaning workers.

syndrome include premature birth, low birth weight, abnormally small head size, facial abnormalities, blunt fingers and toes, developmental delay and learning difficulties, and a range of problems with the functioning of the brain and other organs.

The destruction of the baby's brain cells through inhalant abuse during pregnancy can lead to mental retardation. A 1994 study cited in a publication of the Illinois Teratogen Information Service—an organization that warns of the dangers of smoking, drinking, and drug abuse to unborn babies—found that women who sniffed products containing toluene during their pregnancies placed their babies at high risk for birth defects or developmental problems. Authors of the study examined nine babies born to mothers who sniffed glue. All but one of the babies suffered at

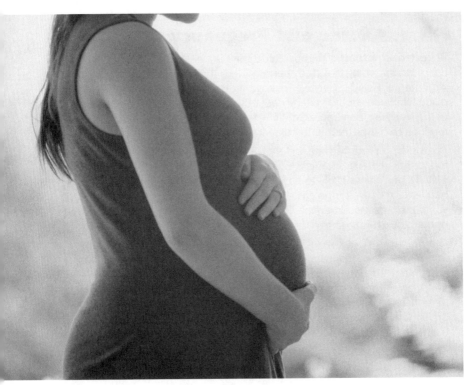

*Pregnant women who use inhalants put their unborn children at risk for
fetal solvent syndrome. This can cause mental retardation, physical
deformity, miscarriage, or stillbirth.*

least minor birth defects. Seven of the babies suffered from some
form of developmental abnormality (physical or mental). One
baby was stillborn—dead when delivered.

In cases where a child is in danger because of his or her parent's
behavior, authorities can step in. In 1996, for example, authorities
responded to a plea to protect a child still growing inside its
mother's womb. In this case, a pregnant Canadian woman who
had already given birth to two neurologically disabled children
and was addicted to solvents faced a court hearing to determine
whether she should spend the remainder of her pregnancy in a
drug treatment facility. The twenty-two-year-old woman had been
sniffing paint thinner and glue for eight years.

During the court hearing in Winnipeg, witnesses watched as the woman walked unsteadily into the courtroom, and they heard her incoherent responses when attorneys questioned her. Members of her family reported that she would sometimes go without eating for as long as eight days. "It's destroying her, everybody can see that, and it's destroying her baby, too,"[35] the woman's sister told reporters. The court acted quickly, ordering the woman to undergo treatment in a residential drug facility until her baby was born.

It is easy to see how the pregnant woman's abuse of inhalants would have adversely affected not just herself but also her innocent baby, whose life prospects would almost certainly have been diminished by the devastating consequences of fetal solvent syndrome. Society, too, would probably have paid a high price had the court not intervened. That price would be measured in the form of large medical and, later, educational costs—not to mention the lost contributions of a potentially productive member of society. But it is invariably the case that the consequences of inhalant abuse affect more than just the user. Young people who huff and sniff exact a great toll on themselves, on their families, on their friends, and even on their communities.

Chapter 3

How Inhalants Affect People's Lives

Huffers and sniffers damage their own bodies and risk death by their drug use, but the impact of inhalant abuse has other ramifications as well. For example, inhalant abuse often leads to poor performance in school or at work. It is not unusual for young huffers and sniffers to lose all interest in schoolwork and drop out. Also, many young huffers and sniffers shoplift to obtain the inhalants they are looking to abuse. Many who become chronic inhalant abusers go on to commit other, more serious crimes that put them in prison. In a few cases, inhalant abuse has been known to sweep through entire communities, swallowing up young abusers in an endless cycle of depression and despair. Many young people fail to realize the impact their addictions may have on their friends and family members. Quite often parents find themselves left to cope with the tragedy of their child's death.

Troubled Home Lives

If young people wonder how inhalants will affect their lives, they need look no further than their own performance in school. According to the National Inhalant Prevention Coalition, young people who abuse inhalants have high rates of absenteeism. They are often discipline problems in school. Their expulsion and suspension rates are higher than those of nonusers, and they get poorer grades and drop out of school more frequently than students who do not abuse inhalants.

One young huffer/sniffer from Ohio, Tricia Hitchcock, told a news reporter that before she started using inhalants she had been a good student who usually earned As and Bs. After she started using inhalants, her schoolwork dropped off and she found herself constantly fighting with her parents. "When school started, I often skipped classes and forged sick notes for myself and my friends," she said. "When I was in school, I walked around in an inhalants-induced haze. My grades plummeted. A friend noticed I liked sniffing markers, so he suggested I make paper book covers and scribble on them to sniff whenever I wanted."[36]

Seeking an Escape

Tricia started abusing inhalants for the same reason many young people turn to drugs: they are experiencing difficulties in their home lives and seek an escape from their troubles through the euphoria of a narcotic high. Researchers report that the worse the young person's home situation, the more likely the young person will turn to inhalants. "Inhalant use is often associated with impaired family functioning," said the authors of a 2004 study published in the *Journal of the American Academy of Child and Adolescent Psychiatry*. "We found a higher prevalence of inhalant use and an increased likelihood of progression to dependence among adolescents with a history of foster care placement compared with those never placed away from home. Foster care is an indicator of a likely history of neglect and abuse."[37]

Tricia did not suffer neglect or abuse, but she was still troubled by her situation at home. Her parents had divorced shortly after she was born. Her father had moved hundreds of miles away, and she felt abandoned by him. Tricia's mother had remarried; her new husband was caring, but sometimes there was friction with his stepdaughter. One summer Tricia tried cigarettes and beer but quickly decided they were not for her. "My parents had

Many huffers and sniffers turn to inhalants as a means of escape from problems at home or school.

no reason to worry: I didn't drink, and I had never taken drugs,"[38] she said.

Out-of-Body Experience

Tricia's life changed shortly after her thirteenth birthday. One day, while visiting her grandparents' appliance store with an older relative, Tricia experimented with an inhalant. The older girl picked up a bottle of touch-up paint and said, "We could get high off this, you know." At first Tricia resisted, but when the older girl inhaled the fumes, Tricia took a whiff as well. "It was almost like an out-of-body experience, an escape from the pain I had been feeling," she later said. "I was lightheaded for about thirty seconds, and it felt good. After she left, I kept sniffing the paint. 'Why am I doing this?' I asked myself. And then I did it again and started laughing. It was a power trip."[39]

Tricia started huffing and sniffing regularly, experimenting with correction fluid, whipped-cream cans, nail polish, gasoline, and air freshener. Soon, she was huffing about six times a day. Her schoolwork fell off, and the one-time honor student began failing her classes. Her home situation grew worse. She constantly fought with her parents. The added tension led to fights between her mother and stepfather; eventually they would separate. After school ended for the summer, Tricia fell in with an older crowd and started abusing harder drugs, including marijuana and methamphetamine. "They never sniffed or huffed inhalants because they were afraid they would get hurt," Tricia said of her new friends. "But I still did, because inhalants gave me a quick high and were convenient—right there in the house or at any store. Several times a day, by myself, I'd sniff or huff nail-polish remover, whipped cream—you name it."[40]

Tricia also started suffering from an eating disorder. Although she weighed just one hundred and five pounds, Tricia thought she was too fat. As a result, she would go without food; then,

Peer Pressure and Inhalant Use

The opening scene of the 2004 movie *Thirteen* depicts two teenage girls huffing from an aerosol can. The girls tell each other their faces have grown numb. "I hear this little 'what . . . what . . . what . . .' inside my head," one of the characters says. "That's your brain cells popping," says the other. Although the scene does not glorify inhalant use—the scene ends as the two girls slap one another, drawing blood—it does show a common behavioral pattern: teens abusing inhalants with their friends.

Harvey Weiss, executive director of the National Inhalant Prevention Coalition, says peer pressure is a big reason many teens turn to inhalants. He said in an interview, "A lot of times, the question comes up, 'Why do kids do it?' and I would say that they learn about it from somebody who says, 'Hey, this is cool. You want to get a quick buzz, try this.' So the natural tendency might be, 'Hey, I'll try this. What the hell?' And so they do it."

Teenagers typically use inhalants between 3 and 6 P.M.—a time when their parents may not be home, Richard Macur Brousil, director of the child and adolescent behavioral-health program at Mount Sinai Hospital in Chicago, said in an interview in *Parents* magazine's May 2001 issue. Indeed, in the *Thirteen* scene, the two girls—who have locked themselves in a bedroom—hastily hide the aerosol can and clean up each other's faces when a parent suddenly arrives home. According to Brousil, the best way for parents to ensure that their teenagers are not abusing inhalants is to see that they have after-school activities and are not home alone looking for ways to fill their time.

when her mother pressured her to eat, Tricia would choke down a morsel or two and then force herself to vomit later. When school started again in September, she argued bitterly with her mother and attempted suicide.

Living in a Cloud

Tricia's story illustrates the type of behavior that abuse of inhalants typically prompts, as well as the impact that such behavior has on the abusers and their friends and family. Argumentative attitudes, eating disorders, and suicidal tendencies are common. Even though young people often turn to inhalants for a measure of comfort, abusing inhalants only makes their problems worse.

Sometimes inhalant abuse leads to truly horrific behavior. In 1998, for example, Richard Marcum of Butler, Indiana, was sentenced to fifty years in prison after a court convicted him of killing his mother. During a court proceeding, a psychiatrist testified that Marcum suffered from a psychotic disorder that had resulted from his abuse of inhalants. At the time of the killing, prosecutors said, Marcum had been huffing paint fumes.

While the actions of inhalant abusers seriously affect their families, abusers often have a wider impact on their communities. Because most abusers learn about huffing and sniffing from their friends, inhalant use can spread from family to family. Young children may see their older brothers and sisters use inhalants and then start huffing and sniffing themselves. They can be expected to pass on the habit to their young friends as well. As Harvey Weiss of the National Inhalant Prevention Coalition explained:

> What's the cost to society of someone huffing? It really becomes a loss of potential. Kids die, adults die, and we have a lot of good kids who are just lost. . . . They start acting out, they start dropping out of school. I think with inhalants it's primarily a human cost. These are perfectly legal products that are being misused because kids are making inappropriate choices, and that's what it kind of boils down to. So you have an enormous loss of human potential, which I think is a great sin, and I think that the potential for so much damage to be done to so many people is mind-boggling. Look at the numbers; there [are a lot] of cases, and the potential is always there for a kid to ruin his or her life."[41]

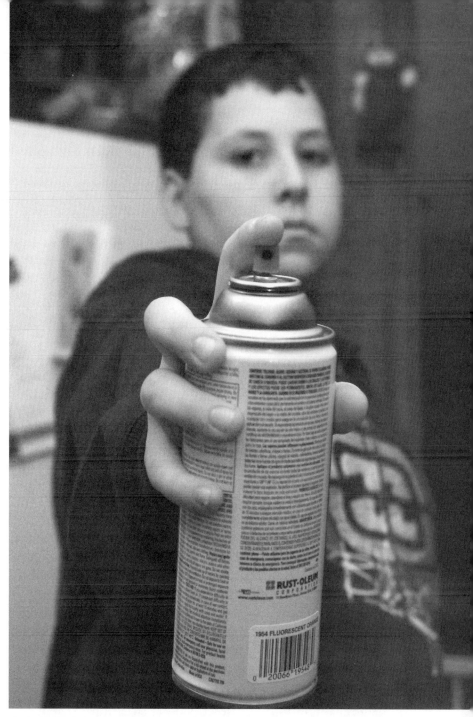

It is difficult to stop young people determined to get high on inhalants, because a variety of products containing the chemicals are present in most homes.

More Girls Are Huffing

Girls have overtaken boys as users of inhalants, according to the University of Michigan's annual nationwide *Monitoring the Future* survey. Results of the 2003 survey showed that among young people between the ages of twelve and seventeen, 181,000 girls and 139,000 boys admitted to experimenting with inhalants each month. In the 2002 survey, boys held the edge by a margin of 159,000 to 143,000.

The greatest jump was among eighth-grade girls. In the 2003 survey, 9.6 percent of eighth-grade girls admitted to using inhalants each month. In 2002, the number of monthly users among girls in the eighth grade had been 7.8 percent.

"What does this mean?" asked Harvey Weiss, executive director of the National Inhalant Prevention Coalition, in the organization's newsletter. "For some reason, inhalant use among females is on the rise while declining for males, and that issue does not appear to be addressed. I have a sense that females are not given strong inhalant warnings because many think that this is 'just a thing boys do.' I believe that young women must be targeted with prevention messages to reverse this trend."

Common Factors Among Abusers

The authors of the 2004 study published in the *Journal of the American Academy of Child and Adolescent Psychiatry* found many common factors among inhalant abusers. In addition to huffing or sniffing, nearly 35 percent admitted to committing some other form of delinquent behavior, such as vandalism or shoplifting. Sixteen percent of the adolescent abusers said they also consumed alcohol, while nearly 90 percent said they had experimented with other drugs. More than 20 percent said they had been arrested. According to the study, "Inhalant use was significantly associated with participation in mental health treatment, a history of incarceration, a history of foster care placement, delinquency, and the use of alcohol and other drugs."[42]

Tricia survived her suicide attempt and spent more than a year in drug rehabilitation. She described her situation: "The whole time I was using inhalants, I lived in a cloud. I lost so much—10 percent of my short-term memory, according to the doctors. Now phone numbers are difficult to remember, and I have to study extra hard. I'll never get that part of my memory back. I also lost part of my childhood. I turned fourteen and fifteen in rehab."[43]

Tricia Hitchcock was lucky because she received treatment and got a fresh start. Inhalant abusers are not always as fortunate. Those young people who continue using inhalants and do not get help risk losing the opportunities that are available to people with a good education and a willingness to work hard. Chronic inhalant abusers face the prospects of dead-end and low-paying jobs, and they have few opportunities to improve their lives.

According to the National Inhalant Prevention Coalition, "Inhalant users are more disruptive, deviant or delinquent than other drug users." The coalition adds that inhalant abusers "have dismal or no future orientations," and they are "uncertain whether or not the future is worth waiting for."[44] Further, the coalition found, inhalant abusers tend to be rebellious, they suffer low self-esteem, and they tend to have friends who use inhalants and exhibit similar types of behavior.

Some inhalant users may ultimately find themselves in prison. Even though inhalants are generally inexpensive and easy to buy, many young people commit their first crimes by shoplifting to obtain the products. Shoplifting may lead abusers to commit crimes that carry more serious punishments. According to a survey that was conducted between 1991 and 1997 by the U.S.

Chronic inhalant users may have trouble finding work that pays more than the minimum wage. Moreover, most users have trouble maintaining a steady job.

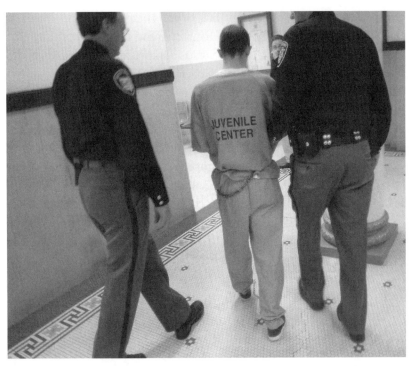

Twelve-year-old Bryan Sturn, shown here being escorted from court, was accused of shooting his aunt and grandmother with a shotgun after huffing gasoline.

Justice Department and that tracked the drug abuse trends of inmates confined in federal and state prisons, more than 14 percent of inmates in state penitentiaries and 7 percent of inmates in federal prisons admitted to inhalant use. Although most of these inmates also admitted to abusing harder drugs, inhalants played a pivotal role in their overall addictions.

The National Inhalant Prevention Coalition points out that because of inhalants' ready availability and cheap cost, they often represent a young person's first exposure to drug abuse. A similar warning is clearly stated in the *Journal of the American Academy of Child and Adolescent Psychiatry* study on inhalant abuse and dependence: "Inhalant use before age eighteen was associated with later use of hard drugs and binge drinking."[45]

Leaving Parents Behind

When young inhalant abusers die, they often leave behind parents and other family members who find themselves stricken with incredible grief. In many cases, the parents had no idea their sons and daughters were using inhalants, so the sudden and unexpected deaths are truly shocking to them.

Even parents well aware of the dangers of inhalant use have been caught off-guard. That is what happened to Dr. Richard Heiss, a California physician who found his twelve-year-old son Wade sniffing air freshener from an aerosol can. As a doctor, Heiss certainly understood the medical consequences of inhalant abuse. He explained that after finding out about his son's problem, he and his wife "spent quite a bit of time talking to him, why he would do such a thing, and what led him to do it, and who else was involved. . . . And we knelt down and had prayer, and we cried and hugged each other, and he promised he'd never do such a stupid thing again."[46]

Two weeks later, Heiss was Christmas shopping when he received a frantic call from his wife, who told him Wade was having trouble breathing. Heiss rushed home to find his son had collapsed on the patio and was pale. "When the paramedics arrived, we worked on him for an hour and a half, en route to the hospital and at the hospital," Heiss recalled. "He'd suffered a cardiac arrest. When we stopped CPR [cardiopulmonary resuscitation] on my son and I watched the monitor go flat, I was devastated."[47]

After a child's death, friends, parents, and other family members must find a way to put their lives back together. It is usually a long and difficult ordeal, and many people never get over the loss. For Tom and Jan Kaye, parents of Brad Kaye, the fifteen-year-old Oklahoma boy who died after huffing butane, the months following their son's death were filled with anguish and guilt. Just walking past the door of their son's bedroom hurt. They blamed themselves for not knowing about his addiction.

Brad's friends, some of whom had known about his addiction before his death, also had to cope with their own feelings of guilt. Susan White, the mother of one of Brad's friends, had once found

Inhaling Helium

Helium-filled balloons are popular at parties. Invariably, though, somebody will take one of the balloons, untie the knot, and inhale the helium. The helium causes the prankster's voice to rise to a high pitch, making him or her sound like one of the munchkins from *The Wizard of Oz*. This squeaky voice occurs because vocal cords vibrate faster in an environment of helium, which is less dense than air. The change lasts for only a few seconds. The voice usually returns to normal after the person inhales his or her next breath of air.

Once thought to be harmless, inhalation of helium has recently prompted physicians and gas industry leaders to raise alarms. For starters, when somebody sucks in a gulp of helium, his or her lungs are deprived of air. Inhaling helium starves the body of air and can make the person black out. Of course, if the victim has other health issues—a weak heart or asthma, for example—the blackout can lead to much more severe problems and even death.

In 1998, a thirteen-year-old boy lost consciousness after inhaling helium directly from a pressurized tank. The boy suffered a stroke caused by bubbles of helium gas in his blood. This condition is similar to what is known as caisson disease or the bends, which can strike scuba divers who surface too quickly. In their case, bubbles of nitrogen form in the blood. Although it was not fatal, the stroke caused permanent damage.

Officials from the Compressed Gas Association, which represents manufacturers of helium, advise people not to inhale the gas. Henry G. Wickes Jr., an engineer who wrote about the dangers of inhaling helium in a 1996 issue of *Professional Safety* magazine, said, "Depending on how completely oxygen is replaced by helium, you may lose consciousness quickly and without warning—you may literally pass out while still standing. The usual result is an uncontrolled fall that can cause serious injury, even if normal breathing resumes before brain damage occurs due to lack of oxygen."

an empty aerosol can in her backyard. When Susan confronted her daughter Kelly, the thirteen-year-old girl told her that Brad had been huffing the contents. Susan White later told a reporter, "If I thought he would get into real trouble, I would have found a way to let his parents know. I was crazy about that kid. But, yes, I thought he would quit."[48]

Jan Kaye explained her many reactions to the loss of her son: "There is denial and anger and acceptance, and not necessarily in that order. I feel cheated that I didn't get to know Brad as an adult. And sometimes I get angry at him, that he'd do that. We have accepted his death, but then again, we haven't. I don't think we'll ever get over it."[49]

Endless Cycle of Addiction

In a few cases, inhalant abuse has grown into more than a problem for individual families. In one such instance, authorities in Labrador, Canada, found inhalant abuse had swept through the entire communities of Sheshatshiu and Davis Inlet, affecting virtually all the young people who lived there.

Nearly all residents of the two rural and remote villages were members of the Innu Indian tribe. In Davis Inlet, most of the Innu residents had fallen into deep poverty and despair. Just a handful of residents held jobs; almost everyone else collected public assistance checks. Suicide was common. Many teenagers growing up in these villages saw few job or educational opportunities or other ways to improve their lives, so they turned to inhalant abuse to escape their troubles.

In 1993, Davis Inlet included only some five hundred inhabitants; the number of teenagers amounted to a few dozen, and inhalant abuse among them was widespread. Authorities there learned of the problem when an angry resident complained to police about loud parties in a ramshackle hut near the town wharf. Simeon Tsnakapesh, the town constable and local tribal chief, arrived at the hut to investigate, opened the door, and was startled by the scene that unfolded before him: six youths, all between the ages of twelve and fourteen, were sprawled across the floor of the shack sniffing gasoline from plastic bags. "You couldn't hear nothing but the wheeze from the bags," Tsnakapesh told a reporter. "Two of them were pretty well passed out completely."[50]

Authorities responded by taking the six gas-sniffing teens into custody and placing them in residential drug treatment centers. The immediate addiction problems of those young people may have been addressed, but when a reporter returned to Davis Inlet nearly a decade later, she found that the inhalant problem had not gone away. When asked how successful police were in keeping youths from sniffing gas, a local officer shrugged and remarked ruefully, "All we can do is put them out when they set themselves on fire."[51]

Journalist Mary Rogan observed young people keeping their arms inside their coats so they could hold plastic bags of gasoline close to their bodies. Occasionally, they would bury their noses below their collars and inhale deeply. In a 2001 article for the *New York Times Sunday Magazine*, she wrote:

> Outside, about 200 yards from the police office, the road was full of arm-less zombies. Their sleeves swung loosely at their sides, and their chins were tucked tight to their chests. No one looked to be more than ten years old. I expected they would run away from a stranger, but they approached me eagerly. When I asked the smallest boy if he was sniffing gas, he laughed and said, "Yeah." The air was saturated with the smell of gasoline, and the children shuffled along in large groups and in lonely pairs. When they spotted the photographer who was traveling with me, they laughed and pushed one another aside to get into the frame, shrieking, "Take my picture, I sniff gas. Take my picture, I sniff gas."[52]

Authorities found a similar situation in nearby Sheshatshiu, a village of approximately two thousand residents. There, young people spent their afternoons staggering along the gravel roads, sniffing gasoline from plastic bags. At dusk, they gathered in groups of fifty or more at campfires in the woods near the village for all-night huffing parties. As dawn approached, the teenagers stumbled home to sleep off their highs. By afternoon, they would get up and sniff more gas, stuck in an endless cycle of addiction.

Finally, parents in Sheshatshiu took the extraordinary step of asking the Canadian government to take their children away. The government did just that, moving twenty-one of the town's young residents—the teenagers regarded as the most addicted to huffing—into residential drug treatment facilities and other living arrangements. Paul Rich, the head of the Innu tribe in Sheshatshiu, explained, "The safety of these children is the paramount issue. The ongoing situation is drastic, and we need to take drastic measures."[53]

Eventually, forty of the most seriously addicted youths from Davis Inlet were also taken to rehabilitation centers. In addition,

Gasoline is among the most abused products because it is easy to find. Many families own gas-powered lawn mowers or other equipment and store small tanks of gasoline in their garages or utility sheds.

the Canadian government erected a detoxification center in the tiny Innu town.

Certainly, Sheshatshiu and Davis Inlet are extreme examples of what happens when inhalant abuse sweeps through a community. Nevertheless, there is no question that when many young people discover inhalants, their interest in achieving good grades and getting into good colleges or finding good jobs is often lost.

Clearly, though, inhalant abuse was already a serious problem in these communities before authorities stepped in. Elsewhere, communities have made vigorous attempts to prevent the abuse of inhalants. Governments have enacted laws, social service agencies have developed prevention programs, and manufacturers' associations have done what they can to prevent the abuse of their products. While most efforts have been targeted at teaching young people about the dangers of inhalant abuse, some of the public education campaigns have been aimed at parents, in the hope of educating them about the abuse and convincing them to keep hazardous products out of the reach of their children.

Chapter 4

Combating Inhalant Abuse

Each year, Congress appropriates nearly $2 billion to the U.S. Drug Enforcement Administration to combat illegal drugs. State and local governments also spend millions of dollars a year on their own efforts to investigate illegal drug dealing and imprison drug kingpins. Additionally, the federal government has signed treaties with other countries, establishing international efforts to wipe out cocaine crops and poppy fields, for example. Yet none of these programs applies to inhalants, because inhalants are not illegal; they are common products that are improperly used.

Even so, attempts have been made to combat the inhalant problem. For instance, nearly every state has adopted measures outlawing inhalant abuse, and trade associations and manufacturers have also tried to fight the problem. Still, drug abuse prevention advocates believe public and private efforts to stamp out illegal inhalant use have a long way to go before they are truly effective.

State-Imposed Restrictions

According to the U.S. National Drug Intelligence Center, forty-six states have established laws to regulate inhalant abuse. (As of 2005, states that have not adopted legislation banning inhalant abuse are Alabama, Arkansas, Montana, and Wyoming.) Despite the large number of states that have recognized inhalants as a danger, however, many of the laws do not provide truly tough penalties for violators. Fines or jail terms are rarely imposed on teenagers caught sniffing the fumes from a butane lighter or a can of computer cleaner. In most cases, a judge will order a teenager caught abusing inhalants to seek drug counseling.

Some laws do impose fines, or even jail terms, on merchants who sell certain products to minors, but Harvey Weiss and other advocates against inhalant abuse have argued that not enough states hold store owners accountable. They would like the states to treat inhalant abuse in the same way they treat tobacco use by young people. Most states have adopted strict laws prohibiting

What Parents Think They Know

A survey conducted by the Alliance for Consumer Education determined that a majority of parents do not warn their children to avoid inhalants. The alliance is composed of several nonprofit agencies and manufacturers of home cleaning products. In 2001, the organization asked five hundred parents whether they discussed tobacco, drugs, alcohol, poisons, and inhalants with their children between the ages of six and eleven. A total of 92 percent of the respondents said they talked to their children about cigarette smoking, while 88 percent said they warned them about using drugs, 87 percent said they advised their children to stay away from alcohol, and 80 percent said they warned their children about the dangers of ingesting poisons. But only 47 percent of the parents said they talked to their children about using inhalants.

According to the alliance, parents generally know that inhalants are dangerous, but they are unaware of the warning signs of inhalant use in their children. They are also not aware of the wide range of products that can be abused. Additionally, the alliance reported that white middle-class parents believe the problem is most associated with minority youths from poor, inner-city neighborhoods, although the evidence shows that inhalants are abused by teens from all social and economic backgrounds. "Parents think they know more than they do about inhalant abuse," the alliance warns on its website. "Parents are far less concerned about inhalant abuse than they are about other substance abuse issues. As a result, inhalant abuse is the least discussed substance abuse issue among those raised in the survey."

Some abuse prevention advocates believe strict laws, similar to those restricting the sale of cigarettes to minors, should be passed to keep young people from purchasing inhalants.

the sale of cigarettes or other tobacco products to minors, and police are constantly on the lookout for retail establishments that sell cigarettes to underage smokers. It is not unusual for police to run a "sting"—an undercover operation designed to catch people breaking the law. In such cases, police seek to catch merchants who do not ask young smokers for identification. Typically, the officers will recruit a few local teenagers and send them into a convenience store with instructions to buy cigarettes. If the youths come out of the store with cigarettes, the police return with a citation charging the store owner and clerk for selling tobacco products to minors.

Although police in some states also run sting operations in search of merchants who sell inhalant products to minors, in most areas police cannot go after a merchant because there are no laws that specifically prohibit the sales. According to Weiss, lawmakers in Texas and California have been vigilant in their efforts to keep inhalants out of the hands of minors. In Texas, for example, store owners are required by law to post signs warning minors about the hazards of huffing and sniffing. What is more, stores that sell butane lighters, spray paints, room fresheners, computer cleaners, and other abused products must pay fees for licenses to sell the products. Proceeds from the license fees go into a fund that finances inhalant abuse prevention programs. However, Texas and California are the exceptions; nationally, few states specifically target merchants.

California stands out because private groups in that state have used the courts to thwart the sale of inhalant products to minors. For instance, the John F. Kennedy Center for Civil Rights, a California-based public interest group, has filed lawsuits against retailers in Santa Cruz, San Bernardino, and Napa counties who violate state law by selling toluene-based products to minors. The suits were filed after the group ran a sting operation of its own, enlisting teenagers to buy glues, carburetor cleaners, bicycle-tire patching kits, and lacquers—all toluene-based products—in several stores. "We're trying to show a statewide practice, and I think we've established that," said attorney Mark S. Pollack, who filed the organization's suit in Santa Clara County. "There is no question this material shouldn't be sold to minors. Sniffing glue can cause permanent damage."[54]

Most national retail chains have policies that prohibit sales of abused products to young people. Often, though, the clerks are not aware of the company's rules, and when a teenager approaches the checkout with a can of spray paint, the clerk simply runs the product through the bar-code scanner and rings up the sale.

Prosecuting Drivers

A handful of states prosecute drivers caught operating a vehicle under the influence of inhalants. As for the other states, they may have very strict laws that subject drivers under the influence of alcohol to lengthy prison terms and heavy fines, but if the drivers are caught operating their vehicles under the influence of butane, that often is not regarded as a crime. In such cases, Weiss said, the harshest charge police can level against a driver under the influence of inhalants is usually reckless driving, which is typically punishable by a fine and loss of a driver's license for several months.

"If nothing is on the books then they're not going to be charged under DUI [driving under the influence],"[55] he said.

Georgia has a particularly tough law that includes fines and imprisonment for people caught driving under the influence of inhalants. Georgia legislators passed their tough anti-inhalant law due mostly to the efforts of Bob Keller, the district attorney of Clayton County, Georgia, and Susan Wilson-Tucker, the mother of a girl who was killed in an inhalant-related car accident in 1994. Jennifer Nicole Wilson was riding in a car driven by a friend who was high on inhalants. The vehicle crossed over the median strip down the center of Highway 85 in Georgia and then was struck broadside by an oncoming truck.

Although Jennifer died in the crash, the driver of the car survived. However, Keller was unable to prosecute the driver for driving under the influence because the state's drunken driving law did not cover inhalants. Keller brought charges of reckless driving and vehicular homicide, but without the drunken driving charge, the penalty was far less severe. In the wake of the fatal accident, Keller and Wilson-Tucker became activists for a tough anti-inhalant law. "Jennifer was just the most happy, bubbly person," Wilson-Tucker told a reporter. "I have this mission for her."[56]

Keller and Wilson-Tucker convinced Terrell Starr, a Georgia state senator, to sponsor "Jennifer's Bill," which made it illegal for any driver to operate a car under "the intentional influence of any glue, aerosol or other toxic vapor." Soon the law was adopted by the Georgia legislature. Wilson-Tucker also convinced school officials in Clayton County to include inhalant education in health classes. According to Harvey Weiss, the "unfortunate truth" about inhalant abuse is that often "the community isn't aware of the problem until there is a tragedy."[57]

No Federal Laws Apply

There are no federal laws prohibiting inhalant abuse. The U.S. Controlled Substances Act has established five "schedules" of drugs that cover substances ranging from ordinary prescription drugs to dangerous narcotics such as heroin and cocaine. The law

Police stop vehicles at a sobriety checkpoint in North Carolina. A few states impose tough penalties on those caught driving under the influence of inhalants.

has established penalties that include heavy fines and imprisonment for illegal use or sale of these drugs. However, this law does not regulate inhalants, which unlike many illegal drugs have legitimate uses. This is a situation acknowledged by the U.S. Drug Enforcement Administration. In material on drug classes available at the DEA's website, the agency states, "A whole group of substances called inhalants are commonly available and widely abused by children. Control of these substances under the CSA [Controlled Substances Act] would not only impede legitimate commerce, but would likely have little effect on the abuse of these substances by youngsters."[58]

Each year, the Drug Enforcement Administration spends its $2 billion appropriation on a variety of efforts to stamp out the illegal trade in drugs. However, none of its money is spent on keeping inhalants out of the hands of young people. Still, there are efforts on the federal level to warn young people about the abuse of inhalants. In 2001, for example, the National Institute on Drug Abuse (NIDA) made $2 million available for scientific research into inhalant abuse. Specifically, the agency targeted the money for studying the physical and behavioral ramifications of inhalant abuse. Also, this federal agency is encouraging scientists to find out whether inhalant abuse is related to race, gender, or social class. The research will determine the best techniques for preventing inhalant abuse as well as methods to rehabilitate chronic inhalant users. NIDA's acting director, Glen R. Hanson, commented, "Scientific research can and must do more to counter the continuing threat to the health and well-being of young people that inhalant abuse poses."[59]

Inhalants in the Schools

Meanwhile, advocacy groups have established programs that assist local schools in teaching young people about inhalant abuse. In 2003 and 2004, nonprofit organizations in twelve states earned more than $8 million in grants from the U.S. Health and Human Services Department to establish inhalant abuse prevention pro-

A middle school student raises his hand during a D.A.R.E. presentation. The D.A.R.E. program brings police officers into the classrooms to teach young people about drug abuse.

grams that can be used by local schools and other groups that come into contact with young people. With the aid of the grants, inhalant education programs are being established in schools, sports and recreation associations, church youth groups, and summer camps.

Yet one of the ironies of inhalant abuse is that many of the abused products are widely available in most schools, the very place where authorities are working to prevent inhalant abuse and where parents believe their children should be safe. Supplies found in the typical art class, for example, may include permanent markers, rubber cement, and cleaning fluid. Students in art classes also may use correction fluid to correct tiny errors in paintings and poster projects. Additionally, many family and consumer science classes feature lessons in cooking, which means there may be whipped cream canisters stored in the class refrigerators. Wood shops contain many varieties of lacquers, thinners, paints, glues, varnishes, and solvents. Hair sprays, nail polish, and nail-polish remover can be found in cosmetology classrooms. And all schools have a custodian's closet, where an array of cleaning supplies are stored. With so many potentially abused products in school buildings, teachers and administrators must remain vigilant about keeping these products locked up.

Parents also have been targeted by advocacy groups, which hope to convince them to keep hazardous products out of their homes and to instead buy products that are dispensed from pump bottles or do not contain chemicals like toluene. Following the death of his twelve-year-old son Wade, Richard Heiss became an advocate for substituting safe products for toxic inhalants. He regularly speaks out about the dangers of products parents store in their kitchens, basements, and garages. "Everything from bathroom spray to markers comes in pumps and nontoxic formulas—you just have to be willing to look,"[60] Heiss remarked.

Drug Tests Fail

In recent years, one way schools have chosen to attack the drug problem is to administer drug tests to students. The U.S. Supreme

Court has ruled that schools can require students participating in "competitive" extracurricular activities, such as sports, to take drug tests. Similarly, many employers now require job applicants to pass drug tests before they are hired.

Usually, drug tests are conducted through an analysis of urine in a process known as gas chromatography-mass spectrometry, or GC-MS. In gas chromatography, a sample of urine is treated with a gas that causes it to break down into its components and stick to a gel coating on the insides of a testing chamber. The next step is to feed the components through a strong magnetic field that

Guidelines for Coroners

The National Inhalant Prevention Coalition estimates that between one hundred and one hundred and twenty-five people die in the United States each year from abusing inhalants. However, this estimate may be considerably lower than the actual total because many coroners and medical examiners do not know how to recognize inhalant abuse, and therefore do not list it as the official cause of death in such cases.

In 2003, the coalition developed a set of guidelines for coroners to follow when investigating the causes of suspicious deaths that could be linked to inhalants. The guidelines spell out how a number of chemicals affect the organs and tissue of a victim. For example, several inhaled chemicals emerge from their containers at subfreezing temperatures, so the guidelines suggest that coroners check for signs of frostbite around or inside the mouth and nose or in the throat. When toluene is inhaled, it causes the kidneys to produce acidic urine, and also decreases the level of glucose, or blood sugar, in the body. When coroners take samples of those fluids, they are urged to run laboratory tests that will search for low glucose levels and very acidic urine.

In a March 18, 2003, news release from the National Inhalant Prevention Coalition, Harvey Weiss explained that once coroners start filing accurate reports about deaths caused by inhalant abuse, human services agencies can use the information to get a better idea of which inhalants are most deadly, what areas of the country are experiencing the steepest death rates, and whether prevention programs are truly effective. "The guidelines significantly add to the knowledge base about inhalant abuse," he said. "The scope of this problem will be better defined. Regional and demographic variations will be tracked. Information derived from outcomes of this tracking will be a valuable tool for evaluating prevention and treatment interventions."

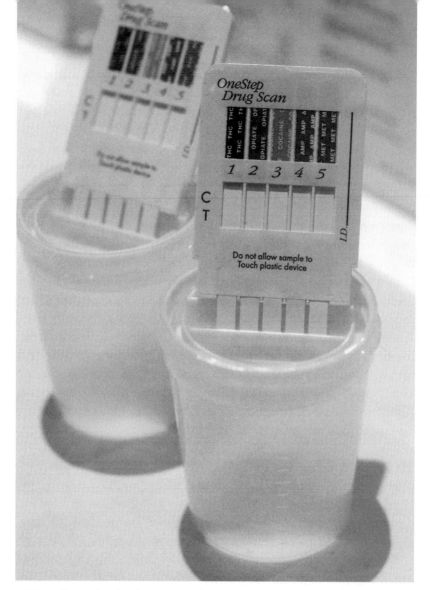

Although standard urine tests, such as the kits pictured here, can identify the presence of most drugs, inhalants often do not show up on the tests.

will enable the mass spectrometer to record their molecular weights. The results of the test are compared against a database of molecular weights assigned to different drugs, including cocaine, heroin, marijuana, methamphetamine, and other well-known illegal drugs.

At this point, however, most drug tests are unable to detect the chemicals absorbed in the body through inhalants. The molecular compositions of those chemicals simply have not been added to the databases used by most drug testing labs. Only recently have some drug testing companies developed tests that can record traces of inhalants, yet those tests still are not widely available.

The failure of GC-MS testing to determine inhalant abuse has led some drug abusers to turn to inhalants to get high. This is particularly true of drug abusers who are going through treatment programs, in which they are regularly tested. They know that taking a hit from a marijuana cigarette or injecting a dose of heroin could result in a "hot" urine sample (one that indicates the presence of the drug in the user's body). To get high without getting caught, the drug user will switch to inhalants. "That's why," Weiss said, "you hear of a lot of people that are involved in treatment will start huffing because your standard urine/blood/hair test will not show inhalants. . . . One of the fears I have is that kids will become more aware of the fact that inhalants aren't being tested for and if they want to get involved in substances, more and more kids might turn towards inhalants."[61]

Efforts by Industry

National trade associations that represent chemical companies and other manufacturers of abused products have made attempts to address inhalant abuse, according to Weiss. Individual corporations have also taken steps on their own. For example, Falcon Safety Products, manufacturer of a computer cleaning product known as Dust-Off, has financed antihuffing public service announcements that are broadcast on television. Also, SC Johnson & Son Inc., which manufactures Glade air freshener, has donated money to produce anti-inhalant videos that are distributed to schools, hospitals, drug counselors, and social workers.

SC Johnson has also printed a warning label on its products that states: "Use only as directed. Intentional misuse by deliberately concentrating and inhaling the contents can be harmful or fatal. Help stop inhalation abuse."[62] The warning label provides the Internet address of the Alliance for Consumer Education, a Washington-based trade association that represents manufacturers

Protecting Workers from Inhaling Fumes

The U.S. Occupational Safety and Health Administration (OSHA) regulates the manufacture of many of the products abused by huffers and sniffers. The agency has established standards for the manufacturers of such products, to ensure that employees of the companies do not breathe levels of fumes that could harm their bodies.

The levels set by OSHA are considerably lower than the levels that huffers and sniffers ingest when they inhale fumes. The accepted OSHA level for toluene, for example, is two hundred parts per million. This means that if the atmosphere inside a glue factory were divided into a million equal sections, just two hundred of those sections would be composed of toluene. The exposure limit for butane is eight hundred parts per million. For the solvent methyl chloride, a common ingredient of paints, varnishes, cleaning solutions, and glues, OSHA's exposure limit is set at five hundred parts per million. By comparison, an inhalant abuser attempts to breathe in a full concentration of the chemical.

To comply with OSHA's standards, companies must invest in expensive ventilation equipment that filters the toxic chemicals out of the air breathed by factory workers.

of household cleaning products. The alliance has established a public education program designed to alert young people about the dangers of inhalant abuse and has made information kits available to guidance counselors to help them establish anti-inhalant programs in their schools.

Weiss said he applauds SC Johnson and other manufacturers for printing warning labels on their products, but he stressed that warnings have limited value. After all, he noted, for decades cigarette manufacturers have been legally obligated to print warning labels on cigarette packs and advertisements, informing smokers of the severe health risks they take by using the products. Despite these warnings, millions of Americans continue to smoke. Weiss believes that teenagers either do not bother reading the warning labels on inhalant containers or, if they do, may simply ignore the warnings.

In one case, a manufacturer asked Weiss whether it would be better not to include a warning label. The manufacturer feared

Warning Signs of Inhalant Abuse

Young people who suspect that their friends abuse inhalants can watch for warning signs. For example, if friends constantly seem to have red or runny noses, they may be sniffing chemical fumes. Sores or rashes around their noses or mouths may be signs of inhalant abuse. Typically, such sores are caused by the caustic chemicals users inhale.

Inhalant abusers often complain of splitting headaches as well as nausea. These are symptoms of someone coming down from an inhalant high. A constant cough also is typical.

Additionally, young people who suspect their friends may be huffing or sniffing may notice a constant chemical odor on their breath or clothes. Since many inhalant abusers do their huffing and sniffing in the privacy of their bedrooms, friends may notice a strong chemical odor there too. Paint stains on friends' faces, hands, and clothes could be evidence of inhalant abuse as well.

Other warning signs of inhalant abuse are similar to the warning signs of more serious drug abuse. Many drug abusers lose interest in school-work, sports, and hobbies and experience an abrupt change in their personalities. They may suffer extreme mood swings or undergo dramatic physical changes, such as sudden weight loss.

that if teenagers read a label warning of the dangers, they might be more likely to huff the product simply to experience the high, despite the risk. Weiss advised the manufacturer to include the label, saying that although the warning probably would not influence the typical teenage huffer, it would give parents important information if they caught their child abusing the product.

Changing the Product and Its Packaging

Some manufacturers have found ways to change either the composition of their products or the way they are packaged to make them less likely to be abused. Manufacturers of airplane glue discovered that adding mustard seed oil to their formula gave the glue an unbearably bad taste. Likewise, auto supply manufacturers that sell nitrous oxide as a fuel additive mix in hydrogen sulfide to give the fumes an unpleasant, "rotten egg" odor. And recently, a manufacturer in the air-conditioning business developed a tamper-resistant cap for tubing that carries the chemicals used in refrigeration. "We came up with the idea after visiting a job site where refrigerant was being stolen," explained Joe Byrne, a representative of Novent LLC, the California company that developed the caps. "There was vomit around the units from people getting sick from the chemicals. We built several sets [of the caps] and gave them to a church, a school district and a contractor who had a problem with a large hotel in the San Francisco area."[63]

Again Weiss applauds efforts to change the content or packaging of potentially harmful products, but he notes that such efforts have limits. For example, when correction fluid first came on the market, it was water-based, so it took a long time to dry. People would dab it on a page and then spend several minutes fanning the document with their hands, trying to get the fluid to dry more quickly. Finally, the manufacturers changed the formula, replacing water with toluene, which made the dabs dry in a few seconds. For the same reason, manufacturers of glue, nail polish, and similar consumer products substituted other chemicals for water. Convincing manufacturers of such products to change their formulas is unlikely. Ultimately, Weiss explained, "The whole issue is not necessarily changing the product, but educating people not to expose themselves to inappropriate use."[64]

And so, despite the efforts of government drug agencies, manufacturers, and advocacy groups, inhalant abuse remains a threat to every person who looks to huffing or sniffing as the source of a quick high. Many inhalant abusers become addicted and find themselves forced to turn to rehabilitation programs to kick their habits. Yet even those who realize they must work to help themselves face a very real difficulty—there are simply not enough programs designed specifically for their unique addictions. According to the National Household Survey on Drug Abuse, some 141,000 inhalant abusers who are in need of rehabilitation are not receiving the treatment they require, and nearly 80,000 of them are teenagers. Young people who do manage to receive treatment face a long period of counseling and supportive services aimed at changing their lifestyles and helping them recognize the true dangers of inhalant use.

Chapter 5

Rehabilitating Huffers and Sniffers

Inhalant abusers who come to terms with their addictions can kick their habits through treatment and rehabilitation, but the road to recovery is long and setbacks are common. While the average alcohol or drug abuser can often complete a detoxification program in a month, the inhalant abuser faces a recovery period that typically lasts three months or more. Compounding the problem is that there are few rehabilitation treatment programs in the United States designed specifically to handle the unique problems of inhalant addiction; in most cases, drug counselors treat inhalant abuse the same way they treat addiction to alcohol or hard drugs. Nevertheless, there are success stories. Many inhalant abusers have started new lives after working hard to overcome their addictions.

Facing Unique Problems

According to the U.S. Substance Abuse and Mental Health Services Administration, just 2,918 inhalant abusers were admitted to treatment programs in 1992, a small fraction of the total population of these abusers. Strikingly, ten years later the agency reported that while the number of inhalant abusers increased, the number admitted to treatment facilities actually declined. In short, the small percentage of abusers getting help has become even smaller. In 2002, SAMHSA reported, just 1,199 inhalant abusers found help in rehabilitative programs.

The decline occurred during a decade in which study after study reported that inhalant abuse by young people was spiraling upward. In fact, the agency's National Household Survey on Drug Abuse estimates that the number of inhalant abusers in need of treatment actually numbers in the tens of thousands. According to the National Inhalant Prevention Coalition, "No other substance has as high a percentage of youthful abusers in need of treatment than inhalant abusers."[65]

Many rehabilitation programs do not meet the needs of inhalant abusers because state and local governments and insurance companies, which fund most drug treatment programs in the United States, have yet to recognize the unique problems faced

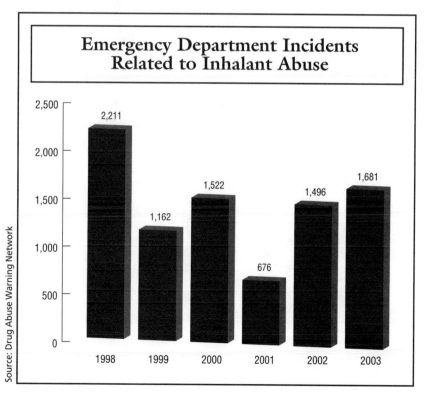

Emergency Department Incidents Related to Inhalant Abuse

Source: Drug Abuse Warning Network

Year	Incidents
1998	2,211
1999	1,162
2000	1,522
2001	676
2002	1,496
2003	1,681

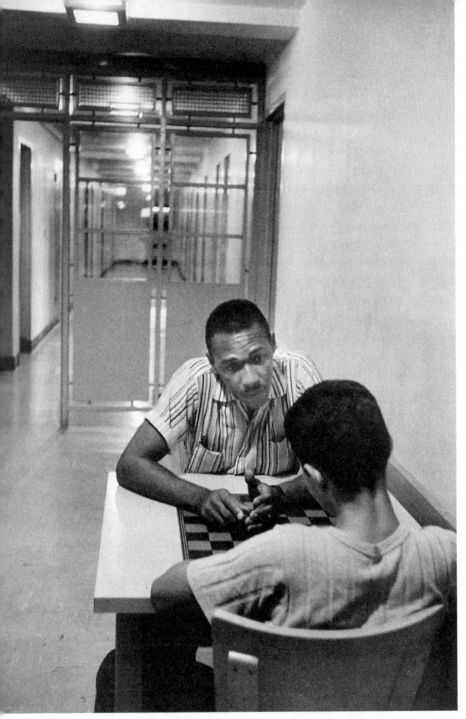

A social services worker counsels a young man about his drug abuse. Often, young people who abuse inhalants refuse to cooperate when forced into drug-treatment programs.

by people trying to kick their inhalant habits. Weiss explained that most governments and insurance companies believe inhalant abuse can be treated like other drug addictions. There is only one residential treatment program in the United States structured specifically for inhalant users—the Tundra Swan Inhalant Treatment Program in Bethel, Alaska. All other residential programs mix inhalant abusers in with their clients who abuse heroin, cocaine, methamphetamine, and other drugs. "Most agencies involved with inhalant abusers do not seem to have a clear idea of the inhalant abuse problem and do not know how to develop an effective treatment approach targeted to this youthful and frequently disruptive clientele,"[66] states the National Inhalant Prevention Coalition in its guidelines for treatment.

Most drug treatment programs are geared to a detoxification program that lasts thirty days because that is how long governments and insurance companies believe it should take for drug abusers to kick their habits. However, Weiss explained that experience has shown that inhalant users take longer to kick their habits—a period of several months in rehabilitation is not unusual for huffers and sniffers. One of the reasons it takes these abusers longer to take control of their addictions is the lengthy time chemicals from abused products stay in their bodies. Inhalant chemicals are secreted in fatty tissue and, therefore, the physical and mental effects of the chemicals stay with the abusers longer.

According to Weiss, there are a lot of people running treatment programs that ask, "'How quickly can I get someone through this?' Sounds a little jaded, but they just want to move them out. [Government or insurance funding] is generally for twenty-eight or thirty days, so that's the goal. . . . Generally, the success rate is not particularly good with huffers. So [those treatment programs are] just not getting the results that you want. [Treating inhalant users is] complex and a lot of people don't want to do it."[67]

Specific Therapies
Nevertheless, some inhalant abusers are lucky enough to find treatment programs that do permit them to stay longer than a

month. South Dakota teenager Megan Hakeman spent three months in rehabilitation. She had started huffing at the age of thirteen and abused inhalants for more than a year before her parents stepped in and forced her to enter rehabilitation. She had been driven to use inhalants after she was sexually abused by a friend; after that, Megan had huffed and sniffed as often as she could. High on inhalants one night, she rode on top of a friend's car, fell off, and suffered a concussion. The next night she fought with a brother. Distraught by the argument, Megan attempted suicide.

After recovering in the hospital from her suicide attempt, Megan admitted to her parents, and to herself, that she abused inhalants. She said, "It was inevitable that my family would learn of my abuse. I couldn't hide it anymore. That's when my parents sent me to treatment for my huffing addiction. For the first month, I hated treatment and I hated my parents. It wasn't until I completed the initial month that I realized this is what I needed if I wanted to stay alive."[68]

Anybody beginning inhalant treatment first undergoes a complete physical examination to determine how much damage the body has suffered as a result of the abuse. Specifically, doctors look for damage to the brain and other components of the body's central nervous system. They also look for damage to the liver, heart, lungs, and kidneys. They search for evidence of lead poisoning and malnutrition, since inhalant abusers usually lose their appetites and arrive in treatment after not eating well for months. All of these areas are checked out because medications or specific therapies may have to be prescribed as part of the abuser's rehabilitation.

Working with Unwilling Patients

One of the first problems facing those running the treatment programs is that clients usually do not want to be there. Most huffers and sniffers have been forced into treatment by their parents or a judge. It is rare for abusers to voluntarily admit that they are addicted to inhalants and need to enter rehabilitation. "When pre-

Young people prepare dinner at a residential facility for drug offenders in San Francisco. Unfortunately, there are few programs designed specifically to help those who abuse inhalants.

sented with a solvent-abusing patient, one is attempting to work with an unwilling individual,"[69] say Colorado State University researchers Pamela Jumper-Thurman, Barbara Plested, and Fred Beauvais, who authored a study on inhalant treatment programs.

Since most abusers are unwilling participants, they usually do not provide drug counselors with much information about their addictions. Often, they are in a state of denial and are loath to admit they have addictions to inhalants; some may not remember many of the details of their addictions. As a result, social workers frequently report great difficulty in getting necessary information on the type of inhalants a client abused, the number of times per week the client typically huffed or sniffed, and the reasons behind the client's desires to get high.

Helping a Friend
Who Has Abused an Inhalant

If a young person discovers a friend under the influence of an inhalant, the National Inhalant Prevention Coalition recommends several steps. First, the coalition urges people not to panic. According to the coalition, people should avoid exciting the inhalant users because they can become aggressive or violent. They should try to keep the abusers calm until the effects of the inhalant wear off; most inhalant highs last no more than a few seconds or a few minutes.

If the abuser is unconscious, a friend should call for help. Cardiopulmonary resuscitation may be needed. While waiting for the ambulance, the friend should search for the item the victim used to get high. That information may be important to the paramedics.

After recovery, the victim should be urged to speak with physicians and mental health professionals about giving up inhalants and possibly entering a rehabilitation program.

Personnel at the treatment facilities will likely request their clients' school records. Since brain damage is common in inhalant abusers, clients may enter drug treatment with some degree of mental impairment, may have become slow learners, or may have trouble uttering coherent sentences. Staff at the treatment centers will want to know the users' intellectual abilities prior to the time they started huffing and sniffing. The clients probably will be tested several times during treatment to measure their cognitive improvement.

Returning to a Healthy Environment

Once in treatment, the clients will be taught how to make effective decisions, how to use their time productively, and how to resist the temptation to return to inhalants. "Treatment programs should be prepared to engage the inhalant abuser in an extended period of supportive care marked by abstinence from inhalants," say the guidelines provided by the National Inhalant Prevention Coalition. "Non-confrontation and an emphasis on developing basic life skills are recommended. Action therapies such as art, music, drumming, dance and activities that involve hand-eye are often beneficial."[70]

Meanwhile, the treatment center will work with the clients' families to ensure that once the abusers are released from rehabilitation, they will return to healthy environments. Problems at home, such as confrontations with parents or parents' own drug and alcohol addictions, are frequently the trigger for teenagers' inhalant abuse. For adult abusers, the trigger may be pressure at work or relational problems. But whatever the case, for treatment to be successful, clients must return to loving families whose members work together to make sure they do not return to inhalant abuse.

Those at the treatment center also will urge the client to make new friends upon returning home. In most cases, friends abuse inhalants together, so it is not helpful for the client to return to the same circle of friends where inhalant abuse may still be going on. Indeed, Megan Hakeman explained, "An important lesson I learned when I got out of treatment was that my supposed friends who I used to get high with only liked me when I was high. I also realized that I didn't like me when I was high."[71]

The Long Process of Rehabilitation

The rehabilitation process is slow. Inhalant abusers often arrive at treatment centers with very short attention spans, because the damage to their brains has made it hard for them to concentrate for more than a few minutes at a time. Consequently, initial treatment sessions may last only fifteen or thirty minutes, so the client does not feel flooded by the new therapy. In their study on treatment of inhalant abusers, Colorado State University researchers Jumper-Thurman, Plested, and Beauvais advise, "During this time the emphasis should be on basic supportive care, including nutrition, exercise, sleep, and a calm environment."[72]

Additionally, because peer pressure is often a factor in getting teenagers hooked on inhalants, many treatment programs also rely on peer pressure to help young abusers kick their habits. To accomplish this, treatment programs usually try to match new clients with partners who have been in treatment for several weeks. The more experienced clients can urge the new clients to do well and help the new clients through the difficulties of entering rehabilitation. In addition, new clients can see individuals similar to themselves progressing through treatment, which should send a message that rehabilitation can be successful—as long as they are willing to work hard.

"When I entered treatment at the age of fourteen, I definitely wasn't the same girl, Megan, who lived next door," Megan Hakeman recalled. "In treatment I learned how to communicate my feelings instead of hiding from them through drugs. That was a major problem for me—anytime there was a problem, I thought if I got high it would go away. Even though I hated treatment for the first month, it was the best thing that could have happened, because I changed in so many ways. Now, I am able to talk about my thoughts and feelings, instead of covering them up."[73]

Lowest of the Low

Many treatment programs also employ group therapy sessions. Typically, the clients sit in a circle and discuss their addictions— what motivated them to start using drugs, what motivated them to seek treatment, and what techniques they find work best in helping them remain drug-free. A drug counselor usually moderates the session, encouraging the clients to speak freely. Such sessions usually prove beneficial for most abusers. Weiss warns, however, that huffers and sniffers are unlikely to benefit unless the group is composed entirely of inhalant abusers. "Inhalant users tend to be shunned by other drug abusers," he explains, "so you may have to sort of set up a program [just for them]. There is a perception [among other drug users] that people that huff are the lowest of the low, and there's a pecking order, a hierarchical structure that a huffer may not fit into. So, it may not be appropriate [for the inhalant abuser] to be put into a group setting with people that have other drug problems."[74]

The drawbacks of group therapy are only another of the problems inhalant abusers face as they work toward rehabilitation.

Once out of rehab, former inhalant abusers are encouraged to make new friends and healthier life choices.

Mostly, though, experts believe that many inhalant abusers—particularly teenagers—have a tough time in rehabilitation simply because they are too immature to truly understand the nature of their addictions or the negative ramifications of returning to their old habits once they leave treatment. Being young typically has another disadvantage for these clients—namely that they are still very much dependent on their mothers and fathers (or other adult guardians) and lack the power to change their home situations, some of which may be quite volatile. Unlike adult drug users, teenage huffers and sniffers simply cannot move to new neighborhoods, find new jobs, and start new lives once they leave rehabilitation. The National Inhalant Prevention Coalition explains in its treatment guidelines:

> Studies on solvent abuse find that treatment is difficult because more treatment centers apply alcohol and drug treatment techniques with the assumption that all chemical dependencies are similar and would respond to these modalities [treatments]. Sniffers appear to have less reasoning and resistance power than alcoholics and other drug abusers due to interruptions in their thought process. . . . Generally, sniffers are not ready for therapy as we now apply it in the typical treatment setting for up to thirty days. The detoxification period in chronic solvent abusers should be as long as possible. Several weeks of close observation are necessary for the brains of these young persons to be rid of the effect of these chemicals. The lack of effectiveness of long-term treatment is probably due to the lack of social and family support, being immersed too early in treatment programs and the reduced capacity of inhalant abusers to understand and cooperate in treatment and recovery.[75]

Researchers have reported difficulties in convincing young abusers to take their rehabilitation seriously and cooperate with their counselors. According to the National Inhalant Prevention Coalition, one study found clients "(1) were not motivated to participate in the treatment process; (2) were cognitively impaired; (3) had low self-esteem; (4) were immature; and (5) generally did not respond well to therapy and other formalized treatment approaches."[76] What is more, inhalant abusers are often disruptive during treatment. They are known to act on impulse, so one minute they may be sitting quietly in a group session or other activity, and the next minute they may be loud, obnoxious, argumentative, and combative. Social workers believe that the best approach is to have a drug counselor work with a client individually. With this approach, counselors may have a better chance of developing a rapport with their clients and of finding a way to motivate them to give up their habits.

Failure Is Common

It is not unusual for clients to resume huffing and sniffing from time to time during rehabilitation. According to the National Inhalant Prevention Coalition guidelines: "Relapse is common among sniffers and recidivist behavior must be tolerated to some extent. . . .The program should require regular 'check-ups' to detect relapses. Encouraging the youths to be honest about 'slip-ups' by reassuring them they will not be removed from the group should they relapse may promote a desire to belong to the group. This would also ensure that members of the group develop trust, a condition essential to effective therapy."[77]

Even after the clients leave treatment, the rehabilitation work goes on. Specifically, clients are expected to return from time to time so that drug counselors can gauge their progress. The counselors also will visit the clients at home, making sure they have

Adults Who Abuse Inhalants

Inhalant abuse is usually regarded as a problem that is largely limited to young people. Studies have found, though, that a significant number of adults are also abusing inhalants. In 2001, for instance, the Texas Commission on Alcohol and Drug Abuse reviewed the causes of death in one hundred and forty-four cases in which the victims were found to have used inhalants. The commission concluded that the average age of the inhalant users at the time of their deaths was twenty-five, with ages ranging from eight to sixty-two.

That study identified Freon, with fifty-one victims, as the inhalant that caused the most deaths. Freon is typically used as a coolant in air conditioners. When inhaled, it can cause the heart to beat erratically. In the cases involving death by Freon inhalation, the Texas study determined that 58 percent of the victims were over the age of sixteen and that 37 percent of the victims worked in occupations that gave them easy access to Freon.

According to a 2002 study by the U.S. Substance Abuse and Mental Health Services Administration, 301,000 teenagers between the ages of twelve and seventeen reported using inhalants each month. The number of adults who reported using inhalants included 150,000 people between the ages of eighteen and twenty-five and 183,000 age twenty-six and over.

Lost Talent

David Manlove died while swimming in a friend's pool. The sixteen-year-old Indiana boy inhaled fumes from a can of computer cleaner, then dove underwater to intensify the high. He drowned.

David's parents, Kim and Marissa Manlove, hope other teenagers can learn from David's mistake. In 2004 and 2005, David's image was part of a traveling exhibit created by the U.S. Drug Enforcement Agency (DEA) and titled "Target America: Drug Traffickers, Terrorists and You." The exhibit details the agency's work in tracking down drug kingpins and shows how narcotics trafficking has financed international terrorism.

Part of the exhibit is called "Lost Talent." This section highlights the toll drugs have taken on famous and ordinary Americans alike. The Manloves gave permission for the DEA to display David's picture in the exhibit when it arrived at Times Square in New York City. Kim Manlove urged people to visit the exhibit to "meet" his son.

"You'll enjoy meeting him and learning about his dreams and the things that are important to a boy his age," Manlove says in a statement posted on the website of the National Inhalant Prevention Coalition.

> He wants to be an orthopedic surgeon like his grandfather. He loves baseball, and has played catcher ever since he was in Pee Wee Little League. . . . Originally, the 'Lost Talent' section was to feature pictures only of famous people from film, art and music who have been lost to drug abuse. Fortunately, somewhere along the way a great idea got better when the decision was made to include unknown people like Dave whose lost talent and potential has been devastating, not only to his family and friends, but to our society at large. Two weeks before Dave died my wife asked him, in the midst of his struggle with addiction, what he wanted to do with his life. And with all the passion and sincerity that only those hazel eyes and that warm smile could radiate he said to her, 'I want to make a difference in this world with my life.' And so you have my son, so you have.

adapted to their new lifestyles and that their families are supporting them. The drug counselors expect to find that the former abusers are working hard in school and becoming active in sports and other community-based organizations. Mostly, they want to see that their clients' time is taken up with creative and positive pursuits, and that they do not spend time alone or with old friends who could prompt old habits to reemerge.

Another problem that faces teenage abusers who have been in rehabilitation occurs when they return to the community and must make up the time they missed in school. Because these teenagers have been living in residential treatment centers for at least a month—and probably longer—when they return to school, they may find themselves well behind the other students. Under pressure to catch up, the teenagers may return to their old huffing habits as a way to cope with the stress. Clearly, it is important for school officials to be apprised of a former abuser's progress, so that they may make appropriate preparations for the client's return to the classroom.

Effects May Never Wear Off

Once rehabilitated inhalant abusers return home, they may notice that some of the effects of their addictions may never wear off. Back in the community, the former inhalant abusers will have to learn to live with some of the handicaps they brought on themselves. For example, the destruction of brain cells may result in permanent memory loss. For Megan Hakeman, a year after leaving treatment, she still found herself suffering memory lapses. "I can't really remember a lot of things," she explained. "When I'm talking I'll forget what I just said two seconds ago. It frustrates me a lot."[78]

Yet Megan is thankful she went through rehabilitation. Now she is looking forward to living the rest of her life inhalant-free. "I was in treatment for three months, and actually, I feel lucky," she said. "In fact, I know I am lucky. Huffing could have killed me. I started to huff when I was thirteen years old. That's too young to do a lot of things, including becoming an addict, or dying. I recently celebrated my fifteenth birthday as a sober, healthy high school student and to be honest, staying sober can be challenging at times. Kids in school definitely huff to get high, and some even ask me to participate even though they know what I've been through. Trust me, I have no plans to ever get high again. I never want to go through that nightmare again."[79]

Megan Hakeman's case shows that a person can give up inhalants and start a new life that is drug-free and full of promise. There is no question, though, that inhalant abuse remains a severe plague on the young people of the United States, causing some to become addicted or, worse, suffer debilitating injuries or even death. Since inhalants are legal, cheap, and readily available in stores across America, there is only so much that parents, teachers, government officials, social workers, and industry leaders can do to keep abused products out of the hands of young people. Only by dedicating themselves to living productive and inhalant-free lives can teenagers truly grow into bright and energetic young adults.

Notes

Introduction: Inhalants: The Silent Epidemic

1. Quoted in "Huffing Can Kill Your Child," CBS News, June 1, 2004. www.cbsnews.com/stories/2004/06/01/eveningnews/printable620528.shtml
2. Quoted in "Inhalant Abuse Rising Among Teens," *Atlanta Journal-Constitution*, September 4, 2004. www.ajc.com/health/content/shared-auto/healthnews/prnt/519995.html
3. Quoted in "Inhalant Abuse Rising Among Teens."
4. Li-Tzy Wu, Daniel J. Pilowsky, and William E. Schlenger, "Inhalant Abuse and Dependence Among Adolescents in the United States," *Journal of the American Academy of Child and Adolescent Psychiatry*, October 2004, pp. 1206–14.
5. Quoted in "Inhalant Abuse Rising Among Teens."
6. Quoted in "Huffing Inhalants Described as 'Silent Epidemic' Among Teenagers," *Fort Worth Star-Telegram*, March 7, 1999. www.mapinc.org/drugnews/v99/n270/a09.html

Chapter 1: A Cheap and Easy Way to Get High

7. Quoted in Woodrow Wilson National Fellowship Foundation, "Joseph Priestley," www.woodrow.org/teachers/ci/1992/Priestley.html.
8. Quoted in "Laughing at the Drill," *USA Today: Your Health*, February 1994, p. 14.
9. Quoted in Dmitri Tymoczko, "The Nitrous Oxide Philosopher," *Atlantic Monthly*, May 1996, p. 95.
10. William James, "Subjective Effects of Nitrous Oxide." http://nepenthes.lycaeum.org/Drugs/N2O/jamesn2o.html

11. Quoted in "The New Kick," *Time*, February 16, 1962, p. 55.
12. Quoted in Edward M. Brecher, "Consumers Union Report on Licit and Illicit Drugs." www.druglibrary.org/schaffer/library/studies/cu/cu44.htm.
13. "L.I. Youths Inhale Glue in Model Kits For Narcotic Effect," *New York Times*, October 6, 1961, p. 37.
14. Quoted in "The New Addicts," *Newsweek*, August 13, 1962, p. 42.
15. Quoted in "The New Kick," p. 55.
16. Quoted in Brecher, "Consumers Union Report on Licit and Illicit Drugs."
17. Quoted in Grace Lichtenstein, "Aerosol Sniffing: New and Deadly Craze," *New York Times*, July 20, 1971, p. 1.
18. Quoted in Lichtenstein, "Aerosol Sniffing: New and Deadly Craze," p. 19.
19. "Explosion Rips Through Garage," Manchester News, December 9, 2002. www.manchesteronline.co.uk/news/s/26/26218_explosion_rips_through_garage_.html
20. "Overall Teen Drug Use Continues Gradual Decline, But Use of Inhalants Rises," University of Michigan news release, December 21, 2004. www.umich.edu/news
21. "Overall Teen Drug Use Continues Gradual Decline, But Use of Inhalants Rises."
22. "Overall Teen Drug Use Continues Gradual Decline, But Use of Inhalants Rises."

Chapter 2: The Physical Effects of Inhalants

23. Quoted in "Spray Paint Sniffers Beware," *USA Today Newsview*, December 1989, p. 3.
24. Milton Tenenbein, "Inhalant Abuse: The Silent Epidemic," *Psychiatric Times*, March 1995. www.psychiatrictimes.com/p950339.html.
25. Quoted in Anita Bartholomew, "Is Your Child Huffing?" *Reader's Digest*, May 1996, p. 132.

26. Quoted in Anita Bartholomew, "Keeping a Child's Spirit Alive," *Good Housekeeping*, May 1996, p. 28.
27. Quoted in Bob Trebilcock, "The New High Kids Crave," *Redbook*, March 1993, p. 78.
28. Tenebein, "Inhalant Abuse: The Silent Epidemic."
29. Quoted in Michael Janofsky, "Fatal Crash Reveals Inhalants as Danger to Youth," *New York Times*, March 2, 1999, p. A-12.
30. U.S. National Highway Traffic Administration, "Drug and Human Performance Fact Sheets," March 2004, p. 87–88.
31. Quoted in Deb Kollars and Elizabeth Hume, "At Least One Jesuit High Victim of Fatal Crash Linked to Inhalant," *Sacramento Bee*, December 18, 2004. www.sacbee.com /content/content/news/v-print/story/11803382p-12691205c.html.
32. Quoted in Trebilcock, "The New High Kids Crave," p. 78.
33. Quoted in Bartholomew, "Is Your Child Huffing?" p. 134.
34. Quoted in Bartholomew, "Is Your Child Huffing?" p. 134.
35. Quoted in Patricia Chisholm, "Does a Fetus Have Rights?" *Maclean's*, August 19, 1996, p. 17.

Chapter 3: How Inhalants Affect People's Lives

36. Tricia Hitchcock and Geoff Williams, "Help Me, Mom, I'm Hooked," *Ladies Home Journal*, February 2000, p. 30.
37. Wu, Pilowsky, and Schlenger, "Inhalant Abuse and Dependence Among Adolescents in the United States."
38. Hitchcock and Williams, "Help Me, Mom, I'm Hooked," p. 26.
39. Hitchcock and Williams, "Help Me, Mom, I'm Hooked," p. 26.
40. Hitchcock and Williams, "Help Me, Mom, I'm Hooked," p. 30.
41. Harvey Weiss, interview with the author, December 28, 2004.

42. Wu, Pilowsky, and Schlenger, "Inhalant Abuse and Dependence Among Adolescents in the United States."
43. Hitchcock and Williams, "Help Me, Mom, I'm Hooked," p. 36.
44. National Inhalant Prevention Coalition, www.inhalants.org.
45. Wu, Pilowsky, and Schlenger, "Inhalant Abuse and Dependence Among Adolescents in the United States."
46. Transcript of the National Consumers League panel discussion, Washington, D.C., January 24, 2002. www.nclnet.org/panel3.htm.
47. Interview with Dr. Richard Heiss, www.drugstory.org/feature/drrichard.asp.
48. Quoted in Trebilock, "The New High Kids Crave," p. 118.
49. Quoted in Trebilock, "The New High Kids Crave," p. 118.
50. Quoted in Gavin Scott, "I Can't Cry Anymore," *Time*, February 22, 1993, p. 51.
51. Quoted in Mary Rogan, "Please Take Our Children Away," *New York Times Sunday Magazine*, March 4, 2001, p. 44.
52. Quoted in Rogan, "Please Take Our Children Away," p. 44.
53. Quoted in Rogan, "Please Take Our Children Away," p. 40.

Chapter 4: Combating Inhalant Abuse

54. Quoted in Cathy Redfern, "Suit Targets Stores that Sell to 'Huffing' Teens," *Santa Cruz Sentinel*, October 4, 2003. www.santacruzsentinel.com/cgi-bin/p/psafe/psafe.cgi
55. Harvey Weiss, interview with the author, December 28, 2004.
56. Quoted in Justin Brown, "Remembering Jennifer," *Clayton County News-Daily*, October 8, 2004. www.news-daily.com/articles/2004/10/08/news/news2.txt
57. Quoted in Brown, "Remembering Jennifer."

58. Drug Enforcement Administration Briefs and Background: Drug Classes, www.usdoj.gov/dea/concern/drug_class-esp.html.

59. Glen R. Hanson, "Rising to the Challenges of Inhalant Abuse," *NIDA Notes*, November 2002. http://www.drugabuse.gov/NIDA_notes/NNVol17N4/DirRepVol17N4.html

60. Quoted in Jennifer Grace Job, "Dangerous Drugs in Everyone's Home," *Parents*, May 2001, p. 184.

61. Harvey Weiss, interview with the author, December 28, 2004.

62. SC Johnson & Son Inc., product precautions for Glade aerosol sprays, www.glade.com/pre_aero.asp.

63. Quoted in "New Safety Caps from Novent Provide Protection from Refrigerant Theft," *Indoor Comfort News*, September 2003. www.noventcaps.com/article1.asp.

64. Harvey Weiss, interview with the author, December 28, 2004.

Chapter 5: Rehabilitating Huffers and Sniffers

65. National Inhalant Prevention Coalition, "Guidelines." http://www.inhalants.org/guidelines.htm

66. National Inhalant Prevention Coalition, "Guidelines."

67. Harvey Weiss, interview with the author, December 28, 2004.

68. Megan Hakeman, "The Story of a Teen Girl's Huffing Addiction," December 28, 2004. www.drugfreeamerica.org.

69. Pamela Jumper-Thurman, Barbara Plested, and Fred Beauvais, "Treatment Strategies for Volatile Substance Abusers in the United States," *Epidemiology of Inhalant Abuse: An International Perspective*. Rockville, Md.: National Institute on Drug Abuse, p. 252.

70. National Inhalant Prevention Coalition, "Guidelines."

71. Hakeman, "The Story of a Teen Girl's Huffing Addiction."

72. Jumper-Thurman, Plested, and Beauvais, "Treatment Strategies for Volatile Substance Abusers in the United States," p. 254.
73. Hakeman, "The Story of a Teen Girl's Huffing Addiction."
74. Harvey Weiss, interview with the author, December 28, 2004.
75. National Inhalant Prevention Coalition, "Guidelines."
76. National Inhalant Prevention Coalition, "Guidelines."
77. National Inhalant Prevention Coalition, "Guidelines."
78. Quoted in Cate Baily, "Pain Meets Poison," http://teacher.scholastic.com/scholasticnews/indepth/headsup/story_megan.htm.
79. Hakeman, "The Story of a Teen Girl's Huffing Addiction."

Organizations
to Contact

Alliance for Consumer Education
900 17th St. NW, Suite 300
Washington, DC 20006
(202) 862-3902
Website: www.inhalant.org

Launched in 2000 by several nonprofit organizations and manufacturers of household cleaning products, the Alliance has established a public education program designed to alert young people about the dangers of inhalant abuse. From the organization's website, students can download studies and other resources on inhalant abuse.

Drug Enforcement Administration
2401 Jefferson Davis Highway
Alexandria, VA 22301
(202) 307-1000
Website: www.usdoj.gov/dea

The U.S. Justice Department's chief antidrug law enforcement agency is charged with investigating the illegal narcotics trade in the United States and helping local police agencies with their antidrug efforts. Visitors to the agency's website can find the agency's book *Get It Straight* available online; it features information for teens on abuse of marijuana, inhalants, steroids, hallucinogens, and other drugs.

National Drug Intelligence Center
319 Washington St., 5th Floor
Johnstown, PA 15901-1622
(814) 532-4601
Website: www.usdoj.gov/ndic

Also part of the Justice Department, the NDIC provides intelligence on drug trends to government leaders and law enforcement agencies. An informative intelligence brief, *Huffing: The Abuse of Inhalants*, can be downloaded from the NDIC's website.

National Inhalant Prevention Coalition
2904 Kerbey Lane
Austin, TX 78703
(800) 269-4237
(512) 480-8953
Website: www.inhalants.org

The coalition works with lawmakers, human services agencies, businesses, trade associations, schools, and private citizens to alert young people about the dangers of inhalants. On its website, the organization provides a number of resources for students who want to learn more about inhalants, including information on the health effects of inhalant abuse and how to recognize inhalant abuse in a friend.

National Institute on Alcohol Abuse and Alcoholism
5635 Fishers Lane, MSC 9304
Bethesda, Maryland 20892-9304
(800) 662-HELP
Website: www.niaaa.nih.gov/other/referral.htm

Part of the Substance Abuse and Mental Health Services Administration, the National Institute on Alcohol Abuse and Alcoholism is primarily aimed toward developing treatment and prevention programs for alcohol abuse, but the agency does maintain a Substance Abuse Treatment Facility Locator. Callers can obtain printed materials on alcohol and drug information as well as the locations of substance abuse treatment centers near their homes.

National Institute on Drug Abuse
6001 Executive Blvd., Room 5213
Bethesda, MD 20892-9561
(301) 443-1124
Website: www.nida.nih.gov

Part of the National Institutes of Health, the NIDA helps finance scientific research projects that study addiction trends and treatment of chronic drug users. The agency's website features many links for young people, including a "Back to School" site that provides students with scientific information about drug abuse and the "Mind Over Matter" link, which explains how the brain reacts to different drugs, including inhalants.

National Library of Medicine
8600 Rockville Pike
Bethesda, MD 20894
(888) 346-3656
Website: dirline.nlm.nih.gov

The National Library of Medicine serves as the medical library for the National Institutes of Health. Visitors to the library's website will find the Directory of Health Organizations Online, which helps people find organizations and agencies that can answer their health-related questions.

Partnership for a Drug-Free America
405 Lexington Avenue, Suite 1601
New York, NY 10174
(212) 922-1560.
Website: www.drugfreeamerica.org

Funded by American corporations and media organizations, the Partnership for a Drug-Free America helps convince young people to stay away from drugs. On the organization's website, several teens and parents have posted their own stories about how inhalant abuse has affected their lives.

Substance Abuse and Mental Health Services Administration
1 Choke Cherry Rd., Room 8-1054
Rockville, MD 20857
(240) 276-2000
Website: www.samhsa.gov

An agency of the U.S. Department of Health and Human Services, the Substance Abuse and Mental Health Services Administration (SAMHSA) helps develop programs for people who are at risk for becoming drug abusers. Visitors to the agency's website can find information on inhalant addiction, school programs, and drug treatment program locations.

White House Office of National Drug Control Policy
Drug Policy Information Clearinghouse
PO Box 6000
Rockville, MD 20849-6000
(800) 666-3332
Website: www.whitehousedrugpolicy.gov

The White House Office of National Drug Control Policy was established to develop a national strategy to combat illegal drug use. Teens can learn about inhalants by accessing the "Drug Facts" link on the website.

For Further Reading

Margaret O. Hyde and John F. Setaro, *Drugs 101: An Overview for Teens*. Brookfield, CT: Twenty-first Century Books, 2003. Covers the abuse of several drugs, including inhalants. Provides information on the health effects of drug abuse and summarizes the police campaign to stamp out the narcotics trade.

Judy Monroe, *Inhalant Drug Dangers*. Springfield, NJ: Enslow Publishers, 1999. Includes real stories by teens addicted to inhalants, and summarizes the dangers inhalants pose to the body and brain.

Kerri O'Donnell, *Inhalants and Your Nasal Passages: The Incredibly Disgusting Story*. New York: Rosen Publishing Group, 2001. Concentrates on inhalants' effects on such body parts as the nose, kidneys, skin, and bone marrow and includes many photographs comparing healthy human organs to organs that have deteriorated due to inhalant abuse.

Clifford Sherry, *Inhalants*. New York: Rosen Publishing Group, 2001. Overview of inhalant use, concentrating on health effects as well as reasons teens experiment with huffing and sniffing. Includes information on where users can find help and how they can kick their habits.

Solomon Snyder, *Inhalants: The Toxic Fumes*. Philadelphia: Chelsea House Publishers, 1991. Among the topics covered are the history of solvents and other inhalants, the effects of exposure on the body, behavioral effects, and how the law treats inhalant abusers.

Works Consulted

Books

Isabel Burk, *Inhalant Prevention Resource Guide*. Richmond, VA: Virginia Department of Education, January 2001. Offers advice to teachers and school administrators on how to spot inhalant abuse by students. Includes information on what type of products are available in art, shop, and cooking classes, and how school administrators can replace them with nontoxic products.

Inhalants: The Silent Epidemic. Austin, TX: National Inhalant Prevention Coalition, 1996. Overview of inhalant use in the United States. Includes information on recognizing warning signs of inhalant abuse, the health effects of abuse, and which products are commonly abused.

Katherine Ketcham and Nicholas A. Pace, *Teens Under the Influence*. New York: Ballantine Books, 2003. Includes a chapter on inhalant abuse, providing an overview of the problem. Includes many resources for parents and young people to pursue for information on treatment and rehabilitation of drug abusers.

Nicholas Kozel, Zili Sloboda, and Mario De La Rosa, eds., *Epidemiology of Inhalant Abuse: An International Perspective*. Rockville, MD: National Institute on Drug Abuse, 1995. A research monogram published by NIDA, the report contains the chapter "Treatment Strategies for Volatile Solvent Abusers in the United States" by Pamela Jumper-Thurman, Barbara Plested, and Fred Beauvais.

Solomon H. Snyder, *Drugs and the Brain*. New York: Scientific American Library, 1986. Describes the physiological changes that take place in the brain due to drug abuse.

Periodicals

Helen Altonn, "Neurologist Sounds Alarm on Inhalants," *Honolulu Star-Bulletin*, April 3, 2003.

Anita Bartholomew, "Keeping a Child's Spirit Alive," *Good Housekeeping*, May 1996.

———, "Is Your Child Huffing?" *Reader's Digest*, May 1996.

Emily Berg, "Inhalants Sicken A.V. Students," *Victorville Daily Press*, December 11, 2004.

Patricia Chisholm, "Does a Fetus Have Rights?" *Maclean's*, August 19, 1996.

K.A. Fackelmann, "The Reproductive Hazards of Nitrous Oxide," *Science News*, October 3, 1992.

Tom Fennell and Nancy Wood, "Horror in Davis Inlet," *Maclean's*, February 15, 1993.

Sam Hananel, "Teen Smoking Down, But Use of Inhalants Increases," Associated Press, December 22, 2004.

Tricia Hitchcock and Geoff Williams, "Help Me, Mom, I'm Hooked," *Ladies Home Journal*, February 2000.

Michael Janofsky, "Fatal Crash Reveals Inhalants as Danger to Youth," *New York Times*, March 2, 1999.

Jennifer Grace Job, "Dangerous Drugs in Everyone's Home," *Parents*, May 2001.

"Laughing at the Drill," *USA Today Your Health*, February 1994.

Grace Lichtenstein, "Aerosol Sniffing: New and Deadly Craze," *New York Times*, July 20, 1971.

"L.I. Youths Inhale Glue in Model Kits for Narcotic Effect," *New York Times*, October 6, 1961.

"The New Addicts," *Newsweek*, August 13, 1962.

"The New Kick," *Time*, February 16, 1962.

Lawrence O'Kane, "City Plans Drive on Glue-Sniffing," *New York Times*, April 25, 1963.

Craig Rimlinger, "Huffing and Dying to Get High," *Fort Wayne Journal Gazette*, July 5, 2004.

Mary Rogan, "Please Take Our Children Away," *New York Times Sunday Magazine*, March 4, 2001.

Gavin Scott, "I Can't Cry Anymore," *Time*, February 22, 1993.

"Spray Paint Sniffers Beware," *USA Today Newsview*, December 1989.

Bob Trebilcock, "The New High Kids Crave," *Redbook*, March 1993.

Dmitri Tymoczko, "The Nitrous Oxide Philosopher," *Atlantic Monthly*, May 1996.

Henry G. Wickes Jr., "Inhaling Helium: Party Fun or Deadly Menace?" *Professional Safety*, December 1996.

Li-Tzy Wu, Daniel J. Pilowsky, and William E. Schlenger, "Inhalant Abuse and Dependence Among Adolescents in the United States," *Journal of the American Academy of Child and Adolescent Psychiatry*, October 2004.

Internet Sources

Cate Bailey, "Pain Meets Poison, The true story of how one teen huffed her way to rock bottom and almost died," *Scholastic News*. http://teacher.scholastic.com/scholasticnews/in-depth/headsup/story_megan.htm.

Edward M. Brecher, "The Consumers Union Report on Licit and Illicit Drugs," *Consumer Reports*, 1972. www.druglibrary.org/schaffer/library/studies/cu/cu44.htm.

Jason Brown, "Remember Jennifer," *Clayton County News Daily*, October 8, 2004. www.news-daily.com/articles/2004/10/08/news/news2.txt

"Explosion Rips Through Garage," *Manchester News*, December 9, 2002. www.manchesteronline.co.uk/news/s/26/26218_explosion_rips_through_garage_.html

Glen R. Hanson, "Rising to the Challenges of Inhalant Abuse," *National Institute on Drug Abuse Notes*, November 2002.

http://www.drugabuse.gov/NIDA_notes/NNVol17N4/Dir
RepVol17N4.html

"Huffing Can Kill Your Child," CBS News, June 1, 2004.
www.cbsnews.com/stories/2004/06/01/eveningnews/prin
table620528.shtml

"Huffing Inhalants Described as 'Silent Epidemic' Among
Teenagers," *Fort Worth Star-Telegram*, March 7, 1999.
www.mapinc.org/drugnews/v99/n270/a09.html

Deb Kollars and Elizabeth Hume, "At Least One Jesuit High Victim of Fatal Crash Linked to Inhalant," *Sacramento Bee*, December 18, 2004. www.sacbee.com/content/content
/news/v-print/story/11803382p-12691205c.html.

Mundell, E.J., "Inhalant Abuse Rising Among Teens," *Health
Day News*, September 4, 2004. http://www.healthfinder.gov
/news/newsstory.asp?docID=519995

National Highway Traffic Safety Administration, "Drugs and
Human Performance Fact Sheets," April 2004.
www.nhtsa.dot.gov.

National Inhalant Prevention Coalition, "Millions Risk Their
Lives by Using Inhalants; Guidelines Tell Medical Examiners
How to Diagnose Inhalant Death," March 18, 2003. www.in-
halants.org

National Institute on Drug Abuse, "Monitoring the Future." December 2004. www.monitoringthefuture.org.

"New Safety Caps from Novent Provide Protection from Refrigerant Theft," *Indoor Comfort News*, September 2003.
www.noventcaps.com/article1.asp.

Cathy Redfern, "Suit Targets Stores that Sell to Huffing Teens,"
Santa Cruz Sentinel, October 4, 2003. www.santacruzsen-
tinel.com/cgi-bin/p/psafe/psafe.cgi

Serwach, Joseph, "Overall Teen Drug Use Continues Gradual
Decline, But Use of Inhalants Rises," *The University of Michigan Record Online*, December 2004. http://www.umich.edu
/~urecord/0405/Dec13_04/mtf_drugs.shtml

Milton Tenenbein, "Inhalant Abuse: The Silent Epidemic," *Psychiatric Times*, March 1995. www.psychiatrictimes.com /p950339.html.

U.S. Substance Abuse and Mental Health Services Administration, "HHS Awards $12 million to Fight Methamphetamine-Inhalant Abuse at Local Level," October 13, 2003. http://www.samhsa.gov/news/newsreleases/031008nr_meth .htm

Websites

U.S. Department of Justice, Drugs and Crime Facts. www.ojp.usdoj.gov/bjs/.

History of aerosol spray cans. http://inventors.about.com/library/inventors/blcan.htm.

BIC Corporation, history of butane lighters. www.bicworld.com /inter_en/lighters/product_history/index.asp.

Pasadena Modelers Association, history of plastic modeling. www.pasadenamodelers.com/HISTORY.htm.

BIC Corporation, history of Wite-Out. www.wite-out.com/about /history.html.

Woodrow Wilson National Fellowship Foundation, "Joseph Priestley," 1992. www.woodrow.org/teachers/ci/1992 /Priestley.html.

James, William, "Subjective Effects of Nitrous Oxide." 1882. http://nepenthes.lycaeum.org/Drugs/N2O/jamesn2o.html.

SC Johnson & Son Inc., product precautions for Glade aerosol sprays. www.glade.com/pre_aero.asp.

"Tragedy in the Household: An Interview with Dr. Richard Heiss," Drugstory. www.drugstory.org/feature/drrichard.asp.

Index

Picture Credits

About the Author

Hal Marcovitz is a journalist who lives in Chalfont, Pennsylvania, with his wife, Gail, and daughters Michelle and Ashley. He has written more than sixty books for young readers as well as the satirical novel *Painting the White House*.

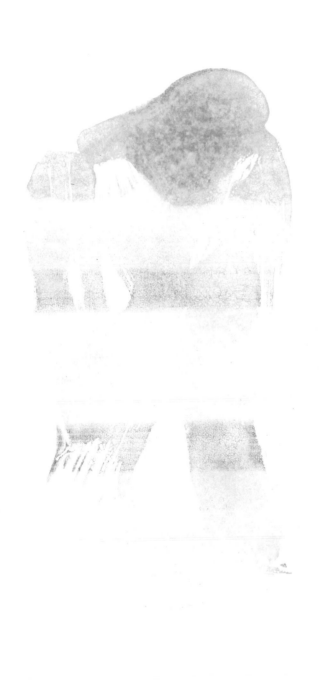